THE BURGESS ANIMAL BOOK FOR CHILDREN

THUNDERFOOT THE BISON. He is commonly called Buffalo. His race has been reduced from millions to a few hundreds.

THE BURGESS ANIMAL BOOK

By
Thornton W. Burgess

Illustrated by
Louis Agassiz Fuertes

LIVING BOOK PRESS

2017

This edition published 2017
By Living Book Press

Original edition published in 1920

1.0.2

SBN: 978-1-925729-01-6 (color edition)
978-1-925729-85-6 (b&w edition)
978-1-922348-29-6 (color hc edition)

A catalogue record for this book is available from the National Library of Australia

Contents

CHAPTER I
JENNY WREN GIVES PETER RABBIT AN IDEA

"As sure as you're alive now, Peter Rabbit, some day I will catch you," snarled Reddy Fox, as he poked his black nose in the hole between the roots of the Big Hickory-tree which grows close to the Smiling Pool. "It is lucky for you that you were not one jump farther away from this hole."

Peter, safe inside that hole, didn't have a word to say, or, if he did, he didn't have breath enough to say it. It was quite true that if he had been one jump farther from that hole, Reddy Fox would have caught him. As it was, the hairs on Peter's funny white tail actually had tickled Reddy's back as Peter plunged frantically through the root-bound entrance to that hole. It had been the narrowest escape Peter had had for a long, long time. You see, Reddy Fox had surprised Peter nibbling sweet clover on the bank of the Smiling Pond, and it had been a lucky thing for Peter that that hole, dug long ago by Johnny Chuck's grandfather, had been right where it was. Also, it was a lucky thing that old Mr. Chuck had been wise enough to make the entrance between the roots of that tree in such a way that it could not be dug any larger.

Reddy Fox was too shrewd to waste any time trying to dig it larger. He knew there wasn't room enough for him to get between those roots. So, after trying to make Peter as uncomfortable as possible by telling him what he, Reddy, would do to him when he did catch him, Reddy trotted off across the Green Meadows. Peter remained where he was for a long time. When he was quite sure that it was safe to do so, he crept out and hurried, lipperty-lipperty-lip, up to the Old Orchard. He felt that that would be the safest place for him, because there were ever so many hiding places in the old stone wall along the edge of it.

When Peter reached the Old Orchard, who should he see but Jenny Wren. Jenny had arrived that very morning from the Sunny South where she had spent the winter. "Tut, tut, tut, tut, tut!" exclaimed Jenny as soon as she saw Peter. "If here isn't Peter Rabbit himself! How did you manage to keep out of the clutches of Reddy Fox all the long winter?"

Peter chuckled. "I didn't have much trouble with Reddy during the winter," said he, "but this very morning he so nearly caught me that it is a wonder that my hair is not snow white from fright." Then he told Jenny all about his narrow escape. "Had it not been for that handy hole of Grandfather Chuck, I couldn't possibly have escaped," concluded Peter.

Jenny Wren cocked her pert little head on one side, and her sharp little eyes snapped. "Why don't you learn to swim, Peter, like your cousin down in the Sunny South?" she demanded. "If he had been in your place, he would simply have plunged into the Smiling Pool and laughed at Reddy Fox."

Peter sat bolt upright with his eyes very wide open. In them was a funny look of surprise as he stared up at Jenny Wren. "What are you talking about, Jenny Wren?" he demanded. "Don't you know that none of the Rabbit family swim unless it is to cross the Laughing Brook when there is no other way of getting to the other side, or when actually driven into the water by an enemy from whom there is no other escape? I can swim a little if I have to, but you don't catch me in the water when I can stay on land. What is more, you won't find any other members of my family doing such a thing."

"Tut, tut, tut, tut, Peter!" exclaimed Jenny Wren in her sharp, scolding voice. "Tut, tut, tut, tut! For a fellow who has been so curious about the ways of his feathered neighbors, you know very little about your own family. If I were in your place I would learn about my own relatives before I became curious about my neighbors. How many relatives have you, Peter?"

"One," replied Peter promptly, "my big cousin, Jumper the Hare."

Jenny Wren threw back her head and laughed and laughed and laughed. It was a most irritating and provoking laugh. Finally Peter began to lose patience. "What are you laughing at?" he demanded crossly. "You know very well that Jumper the Hare is the only cousin I have."

Jenny Wren laughed harder than ever.

"Peter!" she gasped. "Peter, you will be the death of me. Why, down in the Sunny South, where I spent the winter, you have a cousin who is more closely related to you than Jumper the Hare. And what is more, he is almost as fond of the water as Jerry Muskrat. He was called the Marsh Rabbit or Marsh Hare, and many a time I have watched him swimming about by the hour."

"I don't believe it!" declared Peter angrily. "I don't believe a word of it. You are simply trying to fool me, Jenny Wren. There never was a Rabbit and there never will be a Rabbit who would go swimming for the fun of it. I belong to the Cottontail branch of the Hare family, and it is a fine family if I do say so. My cousin Jumper is a true Hare, and the only difference between us is that he is bigger, has longer legs and ears, changes the color of his coat in winter, and seldom, if ever, goes into holes in the ground. The idea of trying to tell me I don't know about my own relatives."

Jenny Wren suddenly became sober. "Peter," said she very earnestly, "take my advice and go to school to Old Mother Nature for awhile. What I have told you is true, every word of it. You have a cousin down in the Sunny South who spends half his time in the water. What is more, I suspect that you and Jumper have other relatives of whom you've never heard. Such ignorance would be laughable if it were not to be pitied. This is what comes of never having traveled. Go to school to Old Mother Nature for a while, Peter. It will pay you." With this, Jenny Wren flew away to hunt for Mr. Wren that they might decide where to make their home for the summer.

Peter tried to believe that what Jenny Wren had told him was nothing but a story, but do what he would, he couldn't rid himself of a little doubt. He tried to interest himself in the affairs of the other little people of Old Orchard, but it was useless. That little doubt kept growing and growing. Could it be possible that Jenny Wren had spoken the truth? Could it be that he really didn't know what relatives he had or anything about them? Of course Old Mother Nature could tell him all he wanted to know. And he knew that whatever she might tell him would be true.

Finally that growing doubt, together with the curiosity which has led poor Peter to do so many queer things, proved too much for him and he started for the Green Forest to look for Old Mother Nature. It didn't take long to find her. She was very busy, for there is no time in all the year when Old Mother Nature has quite so much to do as in the spring.

"If you please, Old Mother Nature," said Peter timidly but very politely, "I've some questions I want to ask you."

Old Mother Nature's eyes twinkled in a kindly way. "All right, Peter," she replied. "I guess I can talk and work at the same time. What is it you want to know?"

"I want to know if it is true that there are any other members of the Rabbit and the Hare family besides my big cousin, Jumper, who lives here in the Green Forest, and myself."

Old Mother Nature's eyes twinkled more than ever. "Why, of course, Peter," she replied. "There are several other members. You ought to know that. But then, I suppose you don't because you never have traveled. It is surprising how little some folks know about the very things they ought to know most about."

Peter looked very humble and as if he felt a little bit foolish. "Is—is—is it true that way down in the Sunny South I have a cousin who loves to spend his time in the water?" stammered Peter.

"It certainly is, Peter," replied Old Mother Nature. "He is called the Marsh Rabbit, and he is more nearly your size, and looks more like you, than any of your other cousins."

Peter gulped as if he were swallowing something that

went down hard. “That is what Jenny Wren said, but I didn’t believe her,” replied Peter meekly. “She said she had often watched him swimming about like Jerry Muskrat.”

Old Mother Nature nodded. “Quite true. Quite true,” said she. “He is quite as much at home in the water as on land, if anything a little more so. He is one member of the family who takes to the water, and he certainly does love it. Is there anything else you want to know, Peter?”

Peter shifted about uneasily and hesitated. “What is it, Peter?” asked Old Mother Nature kindly. “There is nothing in the Great World equal to knowledge, and if I can add to your store of it I will be very glad to.”

Peter took heart. “If—if you please, Mother Nature, I would like to learn all about my family. May I come to school to you every day?”

Old Mother Nature laughed right out. “Certainly you may go to school to me, old Mr. Curiosity,” said she. “It is a good idea; a very good idea. I’m very busy, as you can see, but I’m never too busy to teach those who really want to learn. We’ll have a lesson here every morning just at sun-up. I can’t be bothered any more to-day, because it is late. Run along home to the dear Old Briar-patch and think up some questions to ask me to-morrow morning. And, by the way, Peter, I will ask YOU some questions. For one thing I shall ask you to tell me all you know about your own family. Now scamper along and be here to-morrow morning at sun-up.”

“May I bring my cousin, Jumper the Hare, if he wants to come?” asked Peter, as he prepared to obey Old Mother Nature.

“Bring him along and any one else who wants to learn,” replied Old Mother Nature kindly.

Peter bade her good-by in his most polite manner and then scampered as fast as he could go, lipperty-lipperty-lip, to the dear Old Briar-patch. There he spent the remainder of the day thinking up questions and also trying to find out how much he really did know about his own family.

PETER RABBIT. The familiar Cottontail Rabbit whom everybody knows and loves.

JUMPER THE HARE. The Northern or Varying Hare in summer and winter coat.

CHAPTER II
PETER AND JUMPER GO TO SCHOOL

Hardly had jolly, round, red Mr. Sun thrown off his rosy blankets and begun his daily climb up in the blue, blue sky when Peter Rabbit and his cousin, Jumper the Hare, arrived at the place in the Green Forest where Peter had found Old Mother Nature the day before. She was waiting for them, ready to begin the first lesson.

"I am glad you are so prompt," said she. "Promptness is one of the most important things in life. Now I am very, very busy these days, as you know, so we will begin school at once. Before either of you ask any questions, I am going to ask some myself. Peter, what do you look like? Where do you live? What do you eat? I want to find out just how much you really know about yourself."

Peter scratched one ear with a long hind foot and hesitated as if he didn't know just how to begin. Old Mother Nature waited patiently. Finally Peter began rather timidly.

"Of course," said he, "the only way I know how I look is by the way the other members of my family look, for I've never seen myself. I suppose in a way I look like all the rest of the Rabbit family. I have long hind legs and short front ones. I suppose this is so I can make long jumps when I am in a hurry."

Old Mother Nature nodded, and Peter, taking courage, continued. "My hind legs are stout and strong, but my front ones are rather weak. I guess this is because I do not have a great deal of use for them, except for running. My coat is a sort of mixture of brown and gray, more brown in summer and more gray in winter. My ears are longer for my size than are those of most animals, but really not very long after all, not nearly as long for my size as my cousin Jumper's are for his size. My tail doesn't amount to much because it is so short that it is hardly worth calling a tail. It is so short I carry it straight up. It is white like a little bunch of cotton, and I suppose that that is why I am called a Cottontail Rabbit, though I have heard that some folks call me a Gray Rabbit and others a Bush Rabbit. I guess I'm called Bush Rabbit because I like bushy country in which to live."

"I live in the dear Old Briar-patch and just love it. It is a mass of bushes and bramble-tangles and is the safest place I know of. I have cut little paths all through it just big enough for Mrs. Peter and myself. None of our enemies can get at us there, excepting Shadow the Weasel or Billy Mink. I have a sort of nest there where I spend my time when I am not running about. It is called a form and I sit in it a great deal."

"In summer I eat clover, grass and other green things, and I just love to get over into Farmer Brown's garden. In winter I have to take what I can get, and this is mostly bark from young trees, buds and tender twigs of bushes, and any green plants I can find under the snow. I can run fast for a short distance, but only for a short distance. That is why I like thick brush and bramble-tangles. There I can dodge. I don't know any one who can beat me at dodging. If Reddy Fox or Bowser the Hound surprises me away from the dear Old Briar-patch I run for the nearest hollow log or hole in the ground. Sometimes in summer I dig a hole for myself, but not often. It is much easier to use a hole somebody else has dug. When I want to signal my friends I thump the ground with my hind feet. Jumper does the same thing. I forgot to say I don't like water."

Old Mother Nature smiled. "You are thinking of that cousin of yours, the Marsh Rabbit who lives way down in the Sunny South," said she.

Peter looked a wee bit foolish and admitted that he was. Jumper the Hare was all interest at once. You see, he had never heard of this cousin.

"That was a very good account of yourself, Peter," said Old Mother Nature. "Now take a look at your cousin, Jumper the Hare, and tell me how he differs from you."

Peter took a long look at Jumper, and then, as before,

scratched one ear with a long hind foot. "In the first place," said he, "Jumper is considerably bigger than I. He has very long hind legs and his ears are very long. In summer he wears a brown coat, but in winter he is all white but the tips of those long ears, and those are black. Because his coat changes so, he is called the varying Hare. He likes the Green Forest where the trees grow close together, especially those places where there are a great many young trees. He's the biggest member of our family. I guess that's all I know about Cousin Jumper."

"That is very good, Peter, as far as it goes," said Old Mother Nature. "You have made only one mistake. Jumper is not the biggest of his family."

Both Peter and Jumper opened their eyes very wide with surprise. "Also," continued Old Mother Nature, "you forgot to mention the fact that Jumper never hides in hollow logs and holes in the ground as you do. Why don't you, Jumper?"

"I wouldn't feel safe there," replied Jumper rather timidly. "I depend on my long legs for safety, and the way I can dodge around trees and bushes. I suppose Reddy Fox may be fast enough to catch me in the open, but he can't do it where I can dodge around trees and bushes. That is why I stick to the Green Forest. If you please, Mother Nature, what is this about a cousin who likes to swim?"

Old Mother Nature's eyes twinkled. "We'll get to that later on," said she. "Now, each of you hold up a hind foot and tell me what difference you see."

Peter and Jumper each held up a hind foot and each looked first at his own and then at the other's. "They look to me very much alike, only Jumper's is a lot longer and bigger than mine," said Peter. Jumper nodded as if he agreed.

"What's the matter with your eyes?" demanded Old Mother Nature. "Don't you see that Jumper's foot is a great deal broader than yours, Peter, and that his toes are spread apart, while yours are close together?"

Peter and Jumper looked sheepish, for it was just as Old

Mother Nature had said. Jumper's foot really was quite different from that of Peter. Peter's was narrow and slim.

"That is a very important difference," declared Old Mother Nature. "Can you guess why I gave you those big feet, Jumper?"

Jumper slowly shook his head. "Not unless it was to make me different," said he.

"I'm surprised," said Old Mother Nature. "Yes, indeed, I'm surprised. You ought to know by this time that I never give anybody anything without a purpose. What happens to those big feet of yours in the winter, Jumper?"

"Nothing that I know of, excepting that the hair grows out long between my toes," Jumper replied.

"Exactly," snapped Old Mother Nature. "And when the hair does this you can travel over light snow without sinking in. It is just as if you had snowshoes. That is why you are often called a Snowshoe Rabbit. I gave you those big feet and make the hair grow out every winter because I know that you depend on your legs to get away from your enemies. You can run over the deep snow where your enemies break through. Peter, though he is small and lighter than you are, cannot go where you can. But Peter doesn't need to depend always on his legs to save his life. There is one thing more that I want you both to notice, and that is that you both have quite a lot of short hairs on the soles of you feet. That is where you differ from that cousin of yours down in the Sunny South. He has only a very few hairs on his feet. That is so he can swim better."

"If you please, Mother Nature, why is that cousin of ours so fond of the water?" piped up Peter.

"Because," replied Old Mother Nature, "he lives in marshy country where there is a great deal of water. He is very nearly the same size as you, Peter, and looks very much like you. But his legs are not quite so long, his ears are a little smaller, and his tail is brownish instead of white. He is a poor runner and so in time of danger he takes to the water. For that matter, he goes swimming for pleasure. The water is warm down there, and he dearly loves to paddle

THE MARSH RABBIT. This cousin of Peter Rabbit is a famous swimmer.

about in it. If a Fox chases him he simply plunges into the water and hides among the water plants with only his eyes and his nose out of water."

"Does he make his home in the water like Jerry Muskrat?" asked Peter innocently.

Mother Nature smiled and shook her head. "Certainly not," she replied. "His home is on the ground. His babies are born in a nest made just as Mrs. Peter makes her nest for your babies, and Mrs. Jumper makes a nest for Jumper's babies. It is made of grass and lined with soft fur which Mrs. Rabbit pulls from her own breast, and it is very carefully hidden. By the way, Peter how do your babies differ from the babies of your Cousin Jumper?"

Peter shook his head. "I don't know," said he. "My babies don't have their eyes open when they are born, and they haven't any hair."

Jumper pricked up his long ears. "What's that?" said he. "Why, my babies have their eyes open and have the dearest little fur coats!"

Old Mother Nature chuckled. "That is the difference," said she. "I guess both of you have learned something."

"You said a little while ago that Jumper isn't the biggest of our family," said Peter. "If you please, who is?"

"There are several bigger than Jumper," replied Old Mother Nature, and smiled as she saw the funny look of surprise on the faces of Peter and Jumper. "There is one way up the Frozen North and there are two cousins way out in the Great West. They are as much bigger than Jumper as Jumper is bigger than you, Peter. But I haven't time to tell you about them now. If you really want to learn about them, be here promptly at sun-up to-morrow morning. Hello! Here comes Reddy Fox, and he looks to me as if a good breakfast would not come amiss. Let me see what you have learned about taking care of yourselves."

Peter and Jumper gave one startled look in the direction Mother Nature was pointing. Sure enough, there was Reddy Fox. Not far away was a hollow log. Peter wasted no time in getting to it. In fact, he left in such a hurry that he forgot to say good-by to Old Mother Nature. But she didn't mind, for she quite understood Peter's feelings, and she laughed when she saw his funny little white tail disappear inside the hollow log. As for Jumper, he promptly took to his long legs and disappeared with great bounds, Reddy Fox racing after him.

CHAPTER III
MORE OF PETER'S LONG-LEGGED COUSINS

At sun-up the next morning Peter Rabbit and Jumper the Hare were on hand promptly for their next lesson. Old Mother Nature smiled as she saw the eager curiosity shining in their eyes. She didn't wait for them to ask questions. "Yesterday," said she, "I told you about your water-loving cousin, the Marsh Rabbit. You have another relative down there in the Sunny South who is almost as fond of the water. Some folks call him the Swamp Rabbit. Others call him the Swamp Hare. The latter is really the best name for him, because he is a true Hare. He lives in swamps instead of marshes, but he is a splendid swimmer and fond of the water. When he is chased by an enemy he makes for the nearest point or stream."

"How big is he?" asked Jumper.

"Just about your size, Jumper," replied Old Mother Nature. "If anything, he is a little bit heavier. But because his hair lies much smoother than yours, you probably would look a little bit bigger if you were sitting beside him. As with his cousin, the Marsh Rabbit, the hair on his feet is thin. His toes are rather long and he can spread them widely, which is a great help in swimming. He doesn't have to take to the water as his little cousin does, for he is a very good runner. But he does take to it as the easiest way of getting rid of those who are chasing him. The Marsh Rabbit and the Swamp Hare are the only members of your family in all the Great World who are fond of the water and who are at home in it. Now, who shall I tell you about?"

"Our biggest cousins," cried Peter and Jumper together. "The ones you told us yesterday are bigger than Jumper," added Peter. "It is hard to believe that there can be any much bigger than he."

Old Mother Nature's eyes twinkled. "It is often hard to believe things you know nothing about," said she.

"Compared with these other relatives, Jumper really isn't big at all. He seems big to you, Peter, but if he should meet his cousin, Snow White the Arctic Hare, who lives way up in the Frozen North, I am quite sure Jumper would feel small. Snow White looks very much like Jumper in his winter coat, for he is all white save the tips of his ears, which are black."

"Does he wear a white coat all year round?" asked Peter eagerly.

"When he lives so far north that there is snow and ice for most of the year, he does," replied Old Mother Nature. "But when he lives far enough south for the snow to disappear for a little while in the summer, he changes his white coat for one of gray."

"But how can he live so far north that the snow and ice seldom melt?" asked Peter, looking very much puzzled. "What can he find to eat?"

"Even way up there there is moss growing under the snow. And in the short summer other plants grow. During the long winter Snow White digs down through the snow to get these. He also eats the bark and twigs of little stunted trees. But big as he is, you have a cousin who is still bigger, the biggest of all the family."

"Who is he?" Jumper and Peter cried together.

"He is called White-tailed Jack," replied Old Mother Nature. "And he lives chiefly on the great plains of the Northwest, though sometimes he is found in the mountains and forests. He is sometimes called the Prairie Hare. In winter his coat is white, but in summer it is a light brown. Summer or winter his tail is white, wherein he is much like you, Peter. It is because of this that he is called White-tailed Jack."

"Is his tail as short as mine?" asked Peter eagerly.

Old Mother Nature laughed right out. "No, Peter," she replied. "It wouldn't be called a long tail by any other animal, but for a member of your family it really is long, and when White-tailed Jack is running he switches it from side to side. His hind legs are very long and powerful, and he can make a single jump of twenty feet without half trying. Not even Old Man Coyote can catch him in a straightaway race. You think Jumper's ears are long, Peter, but they are short compared to the ears of White-tailed Jack. Not only are his ears long, but they are very big. When he squats in his form and lays his ears back they reach way over his shoulders. Like the other members of the Hare family he doesn't use holes in the ground or hollow logs. He trusts to his long legs and to his wonderful speed to escape from his enemies. Among the latter are Howler the Wolf, Old Man Coyote, Eagles, Hawks and Owls. He is so big that he would make five or six of you, Peter."

Peter drew a long breath. "It is dreadfully hard to believe that I can have a cousin as big as that," he exclaimed. "But of course if you say it is so, it is so," he hastened to add. "Have I any other cousins anywhere near as big?"

Old Mother Nature nodded. "There are some others very like White-tailed Jack, only not quite as big," said she. "They have just such long hind legs, and just such great ears, but their coats are different, and they live on the great plains farther south. Some of them live so far south that it is warm all the year round. One of these latter is Antelope Jack, whose home is in the Southwest."

"Tell us about him," begged Peter.

"To begin with," replied Old Mother Nature, "he is a member of the big Jack Rabbit or Jack Hare branch of your family. None of this branch should be called a Rabbit. All the members are first cousins to Jumper and are true Hares. All have big ears, long, rather thin necks, and long legs. Even their front legs are comparatively long. Antelope Jack is probably next in size to White-tailed Jack. Strange to say, although he lives where it is warm for most of the year, his coat is very largely white. His back is a yellowish-brown and so is his throat. But his sides are white. The surprising thing about him is that he has the power of making himself seem almost wholly white. He can make the white hair

SNOW WHITE THE ARCTIC HARE. Here he is at home with his friends in the far North.

spread out at will by means of some special little muscles which I have given him, so that the white of his sides at times almost seems to meet on his back. When he does this in the sun it makes flashes of white which can be seen a long way. By means of this Antelope Jack and his friends can keep track of each other when they are a long distance apart. There is only one other animal who can flash signals in this way, and that is the Antelope of whom I will tell you some other time. It is because Jack flashes signals in this way that he is called Antelope Jack. In his habits he is otherwise much like the other members of his family. He trusts to his long legs and his wonderful powers of jumping to keep him out of danger. He is not as well known as his commoner cousin, plain Jack Rabbit. Everybody knows Jack Rabbit."

Peter shook his head. "I don't," said he very meekly.

"Then it is time you did," replied Old Mother Nature. "If you had ever been in the Far West you would know him. Everybody out there knows him. He isn't quite as big as Antelope Jack but still he is a big fellow. He wears a brownish coat much like Jumper's, and the tips of his long ears are black. His tail is longer than Jumper's, and when he runs he carries it down."

"I don't carry mine down," Peter piped up.

Old Mother Nature laughed right out. "True enough, Peter, true enough," said she. "You couldn't if you wanted to. It isn't long enough to carry any way but up. Jack has more of a tail than you have, just as he has longer legs. My, how he can run! He goes with great bounds and about every tenth bound he jumps very high. This is so that he can get a good look around to watch out for enemies."

"Who are his enemies?" asked Peter.

"Foxes, Coyotes, Hawks, Eagles, Owls, Weasels, and men," replied Old Mother Nature. "In fact, he has about as many enemies as you have."

"I suppose when you say men, you mean hunters," said Peter.

Old Mother Nature nodded. "Yes," said she, "I mean

those who hunt him for fun and those who hunt him to get rid of him."

Peter pricked up his ears. "What do they want to get rid of him for. What harm does he do?" he asked.

"When he lives far away from the homes of men he does no harm," replied Old Mother Nature. "But when he lives near the homes of men he gets into mischief, just as you do when you visit Farmer Brown's garden." Old Mother Nature looked very severe when she said this and Peter hung his head.

"I know I ought to keep away from that garden," said Peter very meekly, "but you have no idea what a temptation it is. The things in that garden do taste so good."

Old Mother Nature turned her head to hide the twinkle in her eyes. When she turned toward Peter again her face was severe as before. "That is no excuse, Peter Rabbit," said she. "You should be sufficiently strong-minded not to yield to temptation. Yielding to temptation is the cause of most of the trouble in this world. It has made man an enemy to Jack Rabbit. Jack just cannot keep away from the crops planted by men. His family is very large, and when a lot of them get together in a field of clover or young wheat, or in a young orchard where the bark on the trees is tender and sweet, they do so much damage that the owner is hardly to be blamed for becoming angry and seeking to kill them. Yes, I am sorry to say, Jack Rabbit becomes a terrible nuisance when he goes where he has no business. Now I guess you have learned sufficient about your long-legged cousins. I've a great deal to do, so skip along home, both of you."

"If you please, Mother Nature, may we come again to-morrow?" asked Peter.

"What for?" demanded Old Mother Nature. "Haven't you learned enough about your family?"

"Yes," replied Peter, "but there are lots and lots of things I would like to know about other people. If you please, I would like to come to school to you every day. You see, the more I learn about my neighbors, the better able I will be to take care of myself."

"All right, Mr. Curiosity," replied Old Mother Nature good-naturedly, "come again to-morrow morning. I wouldn't for the world deny any one who is really seeking for knowledge."

So Peter and Jumper politely bade her good-by and started for their homes.

CHAPTER IV
CHATTERER AND HAPPY JACK JOIN

Peter Rabbit, on his way to school to Old Mother Nature, was trying to make up his mind about which of his neighbors he would ask. He had learned so many surprising things about his own family that he shrewdly suspected many equally surprising things were to be learned about his neighbors. But there were so many neighbors he couldn't decide which one to ask about first.

But that matter was settled for him, and in a funny way. Hardly had he reached the edge of the Green Forest when he was hailed by a sharp voice. "Hello, Peter Rabbit!" said this sharp voice. "Where are you bound at this hour of the morning? You ought to be heading for home in the dear Old Briar-patch."

Peter knew that voice the instant he heard it. It was the voice of Happy Jack the Gray Squirrel. Happy Jack was seated on the top of an old stump, eating a nut. "I'm going to school," replied Peter with a great deal of dignity.

"Going to school! Ho, ho, ho! Going to school!" exclaimed Happy Jack. "Pray tell me to whom you are going to school, and what for?"

"I'm going to school to Old Mother Nature," retorted Peter. "I've been going for several days, and so has my cousin, Jumper the Hare. We've learned a lot about our own family and now we are going to learn about the other little people of the Green Forest and the Green Meadows."

"Pooh!" exclaimed Happy Jack. "Pooh! I know all about my own family, and I guess there isn't much worth knowing about my neighbors that I don't know."

"Is that so, Mr. Know-it-all," retorted Peter. "I don't believe you even know all your own cousins. I thought I knew all mine, but I found I didn't."

"What are you fellows talking about?" asked another voice, a sharp scolding voice, and Chatterer the Red

Squirrel jumped from one tree to another just above Peter's head.

"Peter is trying to make me believe that I don't know as much as I might about our own family," snapped Happy Jack indignantly. "He is on his way to school to Old Mother Nature and has advised me to join him. Isn't that a joke?"

"Maybe it is, and maybe it isn't," retorted Chatterer, who isn't the best of friends with his cousin, Happy Jack. "If I don't know as much about the Squirrel family as you do, may I never find another nut as long as I live. But at that, I'm not sure I know all there is to know. I think it would be fun to go to school for a while. What do you say, Peter, if I go along with you?"

Peter said that he thought it would be a very fine thing and that Chatterer never would regret it. Chatterer winked at his cousin, Happy Jack, and followed Peter, only of course, Chatterer kept in the trees while Peter was on the ground. Happy Jack hesitated a minute and then, curiosity becoming too much for him, he hastened after the others.

"Hello!" exclaimed Old Mother Nature, as Happy Jack and Chatterer appeared with Peter Rabbit. "What are you frisky folks doing over here?"

Happy Jack and Chatterer appeared to have lost their tongues, something very unusual for them, especially for Chatterer. The fact is, in the presence of Old Mother Nature they felt bashful. Peter replied for them. "They've decided to come to school, too," said he. "Happy Jack says he knows all about his own family, but he has come along to find out if he really does."

"It won't take us long to find out," said Old Mother Nature softly and her eyes twinkled with amusement. "How many cousins have you, Happy Jack?"

Happy Jack thought for a moment. "Three," he replied, but he didn't say it in a very positive way. Peter chuckled to himself, for he knew that already doubt was beginning to grow in Happy Jack's mind.

"Name them," commanded Old Mother Nature promptly.

"Chatterer the Red Squirrel, Timmy the Flying Squirrel, and Striped Chipmunk," replied Happy Jack.

"He's forgotten Rusty the Fox Squirrel," shouted Chatterer, dancing about gleefully.

Happy Jack looked crestfallen and gave Chatterer an angry look.

"That's right, Chatterer," said Old Mother Nature. "Rusty is a very important member of the Squirrel family. Now suppose you name the others."

"Wha—wha—what others?" stammered Chatterer. "I don't know of any others."

Peter Rabbit hugged himself with glee as he watched the faces of Happy Jack and Chatterer. "They don't know any more about their family than we did about ours," he whispered in one of the long ears of Jumper the Hare.

As for Old Mother Nature, she smiled indulgently. "Put on your thinking-caps, you two," said she. "You haven't named half of them. You are not wholly to blame for that, for some of them you never have seen, but there is one member of the Squirrel family whom both of you know very well, yet whom neither of you named. Put on your thinking-caps."

Chatterer looked at Happy Jack, and Happy Jack looked at Chatterer, and each scratched his head. Each wanted to be the first to think of that other cousin, for each was jealous of the other. But though they scratched and scratched their heads, they couldn't think who that other cousin could be. Old Mother Nature waited a few minutes before she told them. Then, seeing that either they couldn't remember or didn't know, she said, "You didn't mention Johnny Chuck."

"Johnny Chuck!" exclaimed Chatterer and Happy Jack together, and the look of surprise on their faces was funny to see. For that matter, the looks on the faces of Peter Rabbit and Jumper the Hare were equally funny.

Old Mother Nature nodded. "Johnny Chuck," she repeated. "He is a member of the Squirrel family. He belongs to the Marmot branch, but he is a Squirrel just the

HAPPY JACK THE GRAY SQUIRREL. No one knows better than he the value of thrift.

RUSTY THE FOX SQUIRREL. His coat varies from red to gray.

same. He is one of your cousins."

"He's a mighty funny looking Squirrel," said Chatterer, jerking his tail as only he can.

"That just shows your ignorance, Chatterer," replied Old Mother Nature rather sharply. "I'm surprised at the ignorance of you two." She looked first at Chatterer, than at Happy Jack. "It is high time you came to school to me for a while. You've got a lot to learn. For that matter, so have Peter and Jumper. Now which of you can tell me what order you all belong to?"

Happy Jack looked at Chatterer, Chatterer looked at Peter Rabbit, and Peter looked at Jumper the Hare. On the face of each was such a funny, puzzled expression that Old Mother Nature almost laughed right out. Finally Peter Rabbit found his tongue. "If you please," said he, "I guess we don't know what you mean by an order."

"I thought as much," said Old Mother Nature. "I thought as much. In the first place, the animals of the Great World are divided into big groups or divisions, and then these groups are divided into smaller groups, and these in turn into still smaller groups. Happy Jack and Chatterer belong to a group called the Squirrel family, and Peter and Jumper to a group called the Hare family. Both of these families and several other families belong to a bigger group called an order, and this order is the order of Gnawers, or Rodents."

Peter Rabbit fairly jumped up in the air, he was so excited. "Then Jumper and I must be related to Happy Jack and Chatterer," he cried.

"In a way you are," replied Old Mother Nature. "It isn't a very close relationship, still you are related. All of you are Rodents. So are all the members of the Rat and Mouse family, the Beaver family, the Porcupine family, the Pocket Gopher family, the Pika family, and the Sewellel family."

By this time Peter's eyes looked as if they would pop right out of his head. "This is the first time I've ever heard of some of those families," said he. "My, what a lot we have to learn! Is it because all the members of all those families have teeth for gnawing that they are all sort of related?"

Old Mother Nature looked pleased. "Peter," said she, "I think you ought to go to the head of the class. That is just why. All the members of all the families I have named belong to the same order, the order of Rodents. All the members have big, cutting, front teeth. Animals without such teeth cannot gnaw. Now, as you and Jumper have learned about your family, it is the turn of Happy Jack and Chatterer to learn about their family. Theirs is rather a large family, and it is divided into three groups, the first of which consists of the true Squirrels, to which group both Happy Jack and Chatterer belong. The second group consists of the Marmots, and Johnny Chuck belongs to this. The third group Timmy the Flying Squirrel has all to himself."

"Where does Striped Chipmunk come in?" asked Chatterer.

"I'm coming to that," replied Old Mother Nature. "The true Squirrels are divided into the Tree Squirrels, Rock Squirrels, and Ground Squirrels. Of course Chatterer and Happy Jack are Tree Squirrels."

"And Striped Chipmunk is a Ground Squirrel," interrupted Peter, looking as if he felt very much pleased with his own smartness.

Old Mother Nature shook her head. "You are wrong this time, Peter," said she, and Peter looked as foolish as he felt. "Striped Chipmunk is a Rock Squirrel. Seek Seek the Spermophile who lives on the plains of the West and is often called Gopher Squirrel, is the true Ground Squirrel. Now I can't spend any more time with you little folks this morning, because I've too much to do. To-morrow morning I shall expect Chatterer to tell me all about Happy Jack, and Happy Jack to tell me all about Chatterer. Now scamper along, all of you, and think over what you have learned this morning."

So Peter and Jumper and Chatterer and Happy Jack thanked Old Mother Nature for what she had told them and scampered away. Peter headed straight for the far corner of the Old Orchard where he was sure he would find Johnny Chuck. He couldn't get there fast enough, for he wanted to be the first to tell Johnny Chuck that he was a Squirrel. You see he didn't believe that Johnny knew it.

CHAPTER V
The Squirrels of the Trees

Peter Rabbit found Johnny Chuck sitting on his doorstep, sunning himself. Peter was quite out of breath because he had hurried so. "Do you know that you are a Squirrel, Johnny Chuck?" he panted.

Johnny slowly turned his head and looked at Peter as if he thought Peter had suddenly gone crazy. "What are you talking about, Peter Rabbit? I'm not a Squirrel; I'm a Woodchuck," he replied.

"Just the same, you are a Squirrel," retorted Peter. "The Woodchucks belong to the Squirrel family. Old Mother Nature says so, and if she says so, it is so. You'd better join our school, Johnny Chuck, and learn a little about your own relatives."

Johnny Chuck blinked his eyes and for a minute or two couldn't find a word to say. He knew that if Peter were telling the truth as to what Old Mother Nature had said, it must be true that he was member of the Squirrel family. But it was hard to believe. "What is this school?" he finally asked.

Peter hastened to tell him. He told Johnny all about what he and Jumper the Hare had learned about their family, and all the surprising things Old Mother Nature had told them about the Squirrel family, and he ended by again urging Johnny Chuck to join the school and promised to call for Johnny the next morning.

But Johnny Chuck is lazy and does not like to go far from his own doorstep, so when Peter called the next morning Johnny refused to go, despite all Peter could say. Peter didn't waste much time arguing for he was afraid he would be late and miss something. When he reached the Green Forest he found his cousin, Jumper the Hare, and Chatterer the Red Squirrel, and Happy Jack the Gray Squirrel, already there. As soon as Peter arrived Old Mother Nature began the morning lesson.

"Happy Jack," said she, "you may tell us all you know about your cousin, Chatterer."

"To begin with, he is the smallest of the Tree Squirrels," said Happy Jack. "He isn't so very much bigger than Striped Chipmunk, and that means that he is less than half as big as myself. His coat is red and his waistcoat white; his tail is about two-thirds as long as his body and flat but not very broad. Personally, I don't think it is much of a tail."

At once Chatterer's quick temper flared up and he began to scold. But Old Mother Nature silenced him and told Happy Jack to go on. "He spends more of his time in the trees than I do," continued Happy Jack, "and is especially fond of pine trees and other cone-bearing trees. He likes the deeper parts of the Green Forest better than I do, though he seems to feel just as much at home on the edge of the Green Forest, especially if it is near a farm where he can steal corn."

Chatterer started to scold again but was silenced once more by Old Mother Nature. "I have to admit that Chatterer is thrifty," continued Happy Jack, quite as if he hadn't been interrupted. "He is very fond of the seeds of cone-bearing trees. He cuts the cones from the trees just before they are ripe. Then they ripen and open on the ground, where he can get at the seeds easily. He often has a number of storehouses and stores up cone seeds, acorns, nuts, and corn when he can get it. He builds a nest of leaves and strips of bark, sometimes in a hollow tree and sometimes high up in the branches of an evergreen tree. He is a good jumper and jumps from tree to tree. He is a busybody and always poking his nose in where he has no business. He steals my stores whenever he can find them."

"You do the same thing to me when you have the chance, which isn't often," sputtered Chatterer.

Happy Jack turned his back to Chatterer and continued, "He doesn't seem to mind cold weather at all, as long as the sun shines. His noisy tongue is to be heard on the coldest days of winter. He is the sauciest, most impudent fellow of the Green Forest, and never so happy as when he is making

JACK RABBIT. His long legs and long ears show him to be a Hare, not a Rabbit.

THE CALIFORNIA GROUND SQUIRREL. He looks much like the Gray Squirrel but is a true Spermophile.

trouble for others. He sauces and scolds everybody he meets, and every time he opens his mouth he jerks his tail. He's quarrelsome. Worse than that, in the spring when the birds are nesting, he turns robber. He goes hunting for nests and steals the eggs, and what is even more dreadful, he kills and eats the baby birds. All the birds hate him, and I don't blame them."

Chatterer could contain himself no longer. His tongue fairly flew and he jerked his tail so hard and so fast that Peter Rabbit almost expected to see him break it right off. He called Happy Jack names, all the bad names he could think of, and worked himself up into such a rage that it was some time before Old Mother Nature could quiet him.

When at last he stopped from sheer lack of breath, Old Mother Nature spoke, and her voice was very severe. "I'm ashamed of you, Chatterer," said she. "Unfortunately, what Happy Jack has said about you is true. In many ways you are a disgrace to the Green Forest. Still I don't know how the Green Forest could get along without you. Happy Jack forgot to mention that you eat some insects at times. He also forgot to mention that sometimes you have a storehouse down in the ground. Now tell us what you know about your cousin, Happy Jack."

For a few minutes Chatterer sulked, but he did not dare disobey Old Mother Nature. "I don't know much good about him," he mumbled.

"And you don't know much bad about me either," retorted Happy Jack sharply.

Old Mother Nature held up a warning hand. "That will do," said she. "Now, Chatterer, go on."

"Happy Jack is more than twice as big as I, but at that, I'm not afraid of him," said Chatterer and glared at Happy Jack. "He is gray all over, except underneath, where he is white. He has a tremendously big tail and is so proud of it he shows it off whenever he has a chance. When he sits up he has a way of folding his hands on his breast. I don't know what he does it for unless it is to keep them warm in cold weather. He builds a nest very much like mine.

Sometimes it is in a hollow tree, but quite as often it is in the branches of a tree. He is a good traveler in the treetops, but he spends a good deal of his time on the ground. He likes open woodland best, especially where there are many nut trees. He has a storehouse where he stores up nuts for winter, but he buries in the ground and under the leaves more than he puts in his storehouse. In winter, when he is hungry, he hunts for those buried nuts, and somehow he manages to find them even when they are covered with snow. When he comes to stealing he is not better than I am. I have seen him steal birds' eggs, and I wouldn't trust him unwatched around one of my storehouses."

It was Happy Jacks' turn to become indignant. "I may have taken a few eggs when I accidentally ran across them," said he, "but I never go looking for them, and I don't take them unless I am very hungry and can't find anything else. I don't make a business of robbing birds the way you do, and you know it. If I find one of your storehouses and help myself, I am only getting back what you have stolen from me. Everybody loves me and that is more than you can say."

"That's enough," declared Old Mother Nature, and her voice was very sharp. "You two cousins never have agreed and I am afraid never will. As long as you are neighbors, I suspect you will quarrel. Have you told us all you know about Happy Jack, Chatterer?"

Chatterer nodded. He was still mumbling to himself angrily and wasn't polite enough to make a reply. Old Mother Nature took no notice of this. "What you have told us is good as far as it goes," said she. "You said that Happy Jack is all gray excepting underneath. Usually the Gray Squirrel is just as Chatterer has described him, but sometimes a Gray Squirrel isn't gray at all, but all black."

Peter Rabbit's ears stood straight up with astonishment. "How can a Gray Squirrel be black?" he demanded.

Old Mother Nature smiled. "That is a fair question, Peter," said she. "Gray Squirrel is simply the name of Happy Jack's family. Sometimes some of the babies are born with black coats instead of gray coats. Of course they are just the same kind of Squirrel, only they look different. In some parts of the country there are numbers of these black-coated Squirrels and many think they are a different kind of Squirrel. They are not. They are simply black-coated members of Happy Jack's family. Just remember this. It is the same way in the family of Rusty the Fox Squirrel. Some members are rusty red, some are a mixture of red and gray, and some are as gray as Happy Jack himself. Way down in the Sunny South Fox Squirrels always have white noses and ears. In the North they never have white noses and ears. Rusty the Fox Squirrel is just a little bigger than Happy Jack and has just such a handsome tail. He is the strongest and heaviest of the Tree Squirrels and not nearly as quick and graceful as Happy Jack. Sometimes Rusty has two nests in the same tree, one in a hollow in a tree for bad weather and the other made of sticks and leaves outside in the branches for use in good weather. Rusty's habits are very much the same as those of Happy Jack the Gray Squirrel, and therefore he likes the same kind of surroundings. Like his cousin, Happy Jack, Rusty is a great help to me."

Seeing how surprised everybody looked, Mother Nature explained. "Both Happy Jack and Rusty bury a great many more nuts than they ever need," said she, "and those they do not dig up sprout in the spring and grow. In that way they plant ever so many trees without knowing it. Just remember that, Chatterer, the next time you are tempted to quarrel with your cousin, Happy Jack. Very likely Happy Jack's great-great-ever-so-great grandfather planted the very tree you get your fattest and best hickory nuts from.

"Way out in the mountains of the Far West you have a cousin called the Douglas Squirrel, who is really a true Red Squirrel and whose habits are very much like your own. Some folks call him the Pine Squirrel. By the way, Chatterer, Happy Jack forgot to say that you are a good swimmer. Perhaps he didn't know it."

By the expression of Happy Jack's face it was quite clear

that he didn't know it. "Certainly I can swim," said Chatterer. "I don't mind the water at all. I can swim a long distance if I have to."

This was quite as much news to Peter Rabbit as had been the fact that a cousin of his own was a good swimmer, and he began to feel something very like respect for Chatterer.

"Are there any other Tree Squirrels?" asked Jumper the Hare.

"Yes," replied Old Mother Nature, "there are two—the handsomest of all the family. They live out in the Southwest, in one of the most wonderful places in all this great land, a place called the Grand Canyon. One is called the Abert Squirrel and the other the Kaibab Squirrel. They are about the size of Happy Jack and Rusty but have broader, handsomer tails and their ears have long tufts of hair. The Abert Squirrel has black ears, a brown back, gray sides and white underneath. Kaibab has brown ears with black tips, and his tail is mostly white. Both are very lovely, but their families are small and so they are little known."

With this, Old Mother Nature dismissed school for the day.

CHAPTER VI
STRIPED CHIPMUNK AND HIS COUSINS

Of course there couldn't be a school in the Green Forest without news of it spreading very fast. News travels quickly through the Green Forest and over the Green Meadows, for the little people who live there are great gossips. So it was not surprising that Striped Chipmunk heard all about Old Mother Nature's school. The next morning, just as the daily lesson was beginning, Striped Chipmunk came hurrying up, quite out of breath.

"Well, well! See who's here!" exclaimed Old Mother Nature. "What have you come for, Striped Chipmunk?"

"I've come to try to learn. Will you let me stay, Mother Nature?" replied Striped Chipmunk.

"Of course I'll let you stay," cried Old Mother Nature heartily. "I am glad you have come, especially glad you have come today, because to-day's lesson is to be about you and your cousins. Now, Peter Rabbit, what are the differences between Striped Chipmunk and his cousins, the Tree Squirrels?"

Peter looked very hard at Striped Chipmunk as if he had never really seen him before. "He is smaller than they are," began Peter. "In fact, he is the smallest Squirrel I know." Peter paused.

Old Mother Nature nodded encouragingly. "Go on," said she.

"He wears a striped coat," continued Peter. "The stripes are black and yellowish-white and run along his sides, a black stripe running down the middle of his back. The rest of his coat is reddish-brown above and light underneath. His tail is rather thin and flat. I never see him in the trees, so I guess he can't climb."

"Oh, yes, I can," interrupted Striped Chipmunk. "I can climb if I want to, and I do sometimes, but prefer the ground."

"Go on, Peter," said Old Mother Nature.

"He seems to like old stone walls and rock piles," continued Peter, "and he is one of the brightest, liveliest, merriest and the most lovable of all my friends."

"Thank you, Peter," said Striped Chipmunk softly.

"I never have been able to find his home," continued Peter. "That is one of his secrets. But I know it is in the ground. I guess this is all I know about him. I should say the chief difference between Striped Chipmunk and the Tree Squirrels is that he spends all his time on the ground while the others live largely in the trees."

"Very good, Peter," said Old Mother Nature. "But there are two very important differences which you have not mentioned. Striped Chipmunk has a big pocket on the inside of each cheek, while his cousins of the trees have no pockets at all."

"Of course," cried Peter. "I don't see how I came to forget that. I've laughed many times at Striped Chipmunk with those pockets stuffed with nuts or seeds until his head looked three times bigger than it does now. Those pockets must be very handy."

"They are," replied Striped Chipmunk. "I couldn't get along without them. They save me a lot of running back and forth, I can tell you."

"And the other great difference," said Old Mother Nature, "is that Striped Chipmunk sleeps nearly all winter, just waking up occasionally to pop his head out on a bright day to see how the weather is. A great many folks call Striped Chipmunk a Ground Squirrel, but more properly he is a Rock Squirrel because he likes stony places best. Supposing, Striped Chipmunk, you tell us where and how you make your home."

"I make my home down in the ground," replied Striped Chipmunk. "I dig a tunnel just big enough to run along comfortably. Down deep enough to be out of reach of Jack Frost I make a nice little bedroom with a bed of grass and leaves, and I make another little room for a storeroom in which to keep my supply of seeds and nuts. Sometimes I

TIMMY THE FLYING SQUIRREL. He does not actually fly for he has no wings.

CHATTERER THE RED SQUIRREL. The little rollicking mischief-maker of the Green Forest.

have more than one storeroom. Also I have some little side tunnels."

"But why is it I never have been able to find the entrance to your tunnel?" asked Peter, as full of curiosity as ever.

"Because I have it hidden underneath the stone wall on the edge of the Old Orchard," replied Striped Chipmunk.

"But even then, I should think that all the sand you must have taken out would give your secret away," cried Peter.

Striped Chipmunk chuckled happily. It was a throaty little chuckle, pleasant to hear. "I looked out for that," said he. "There isn't a grain of that sand around my doorway. I took it all out through another hole some distance away, a sort of back door, and then closed it up solidly. If you please, Mother Nature, if I am not a Ground Squirrel, who is?"

"Your cousin, Seek Seek the Spermophile, sometimes called Gopher Squirrel, who lives on the open plains of the West where there are no rocks or stones. He likes best the flat, open country. He is called Spermophile because that means seed-eater, and he lives largely on seeds, especially on grain. Because of this he does a great deal of damage and is much disliked by farmers.

"Seek Seek's family are the true Ground Squirrels. Please remember that they never should be called Gophers, for they are not Gophers. One of the smallest members of the family is just about your size, Striped Chipmunk, and he also wears stripes, only he has more of them than you have, and they are broken up into little dots. He is called the Thirteen-lined Spermophile. He has pockets in his cheeks just as you have, and he makes a home down in the ground very similar to yours. All the family do this, and all of them sleep through the winter. While they are great seed-eaters they also eat a great many insects and worms, and some of them even are guilty of killing and eating the babies of birds that nest on the ground, and also young mice.

"Some members of the family are almost as big as Happy Jack the Gray Squirrel and have gray coats. They are called Gray Ground Squirrels and sometimes Gray Gophers. One of the largest of these is the California Ground Squirrel. He has a big, bushy tail, very like Happy Jack's. He gets into so much mischief in the grain fields and in the orchards that he is quite as much disliked as is Jack Rabbit. This particular member of the family is quite as much at home among rocks and tree roots as in open ground. He climbs low trees for fruit and nuts, but prefers to stay on the ground. Now just remember that the Chipmunks are Rock Squirrels and their cousins the Spermophiles are Ground Squirrels. Now who of you has seen Timmy the Flying Squirrel lately?"

"I haven't," said Peter Rabbit.

"I haven't," said Striped Chipmunk.

"I haven't," said Happy Jack.

"I haven't," said Chatterer.

"I have," spoke up Jumper the Hare. "I saw him last evening just after jolly, round, red Mr. Sun went to bed behind the Purple Hills and the Black Shadows came creeping through the Green Forest. My, I wish I could fly the way he can!"

Old Mother Nature shook her head disapprovingly. "Jumper," said she, "what is wrong with your eyes? When did you ever see Timmy fly?"

"Last night," insisted Jumper stubbornly.

"Oh, no, you didn't," retorted Old Mother Nature. "You didn't see him fly, for the very good reason that he cannot fly any more than you can. You saw him simply jump. Just remember that the only animals in this great land who can fly are the Bats. Timmy the Flying Squirrel simply jumps from the top of a tree and slides down on the air to the foot of another tree. If you had used your eyes you would have noticed that when he is in the air he never moves his legs or arms, and he is always coming down, never going up, excepting for a little at the end of his jump, as would be the case if he could really fly. He hasn't any wings."

"When he's flying, I mean jumping, he looks as if he had wings," insisted Jumper stubbornly.

"That is simply because I have given him a fold of skin between the front and hind leg on each side," explained Old Mother Nature. "When he jumps he stretches his legs out flat, and that stretches out those two folds of skin until they look almost like wings. This is the reason he can sail so far when he jumps from a high place. You've seen a bird, after flapping its wings to get going, sail along with them outstretched and motionless. Timmy does the same thing, only he gets going by jumping. You may have noticed that he usually goes to the top of a tree before jumping; then he can sail down a wonderfully long distance. His tail helps him to keep his balance. If there is anything in the way, he can steer himself around it. When he reaches the tree he is jumping for he shoots up a little way and lands on the trunk not far above the ground. Then he scampers up that tree to do it all over again."

"But why don't we ever see him?" inquired Striped Chipmunk.

"Because, when the rest of you squirrels are out and about, he is curled up in a little ball in his nest, fast asleep. Timmy likes the night, especially the early evening, and doesn't like the light of day."

"How big is he?" asked Happy Jack, and looked a little sheepish as if he were a wee bit ashamed of not being acquainted with one of his own cousins.

"He is, if anything, a little smaller than Striped Chipmunk," replied Old Mother Nature. "Way out in the Far West he grows a little bigger. His coat is a soft yellowish-brown above; beneath he is all white. His fur is wonderfully soft. He has very large, dark, soft eyes, especially suited for seeing at night. Then, he is very lively and dearly loves to play. By nature he is gentle and lovable."

"Does he eat nuts like his cousins?" asked Peter Rabbit.

"He certainly does," replied Old Mother Nature. "Also he eats grubs and insects. He dearly loves a fat beetle. He likes meat when he can get it."

STRIPED CHIPMUNK. He has pockets in his cheeks for carrying his food.

SEEK SEEK THE SPERMOPHILE. The Thirteen-lined Spermophile, a true Ground Squirrel and not a Gopher.

"Where does he make his home?" Peter inquired.

"Usually in a hole in a tree," said Old Mother Nature. "He is very fond of an old home of a Woodpecker. He makes a comfortable nest of bark lining, grass, and moss, or any other soft material he can find. Occasionally he builds an outside nest high up in a fork in the branches of a tree. He likes to get into old buildings."

"Does he have many enemies?" asked Happy Jack.

"The same enemies the rest of you have," replied Old Mother Nature. "But the one he has most reason to fear is Hooty the Owl, and that is the one you have least reason to fear, because Hooty seldom hunts by day."

"Does he sleep all winter?" piped up Striped Chipmunk.

"Not as you do," said Old Mother Nature. "In very cold weather he sleeps, but if he happens to be living where the weather does not get very cold, he is active all the year around. Now I guess this is enough about the Squirrel family."

"You've forgotten Johnny Chuck," cried Peter.

Old Mother Nature laughed. "So I have," said she. "That will never do, never in the world. Johnny and his relatives, the Marmots, certainly cannot be overlooked. We will take them for our lesson to-morrow. Peter, you tell Johnny Chuck to come over here to-morrow morning."

CHAPTER VII
JOHNNY CHUCK JOINS THE CLASS

Peter Rabbit delivered Mother Nature's message to Johnny Chuck. Johnny didn't seem at all pleased. He grumbled and growled to himself. He didn't want to go to school. He didn't want to learn anything about his relatives. He was perfectly satisfied with things as they were. The truth is, Johnny Chuck was already beginning to get fat with good living and he is naturally lazy. As a rule he can find plenty to eat very near his home, so he seldom goes far from his own doorstep. Peter left him grumbling and growling, and chuckled to himself all the way back to the dear Old Briar-patch. He knew that Johnny Chuck would not dare disobey Old Mother Nature.

Sure enough, the next morning Johnny Chuck came waddling through the Green Forest just as Old Mother Nature was about to open school. He didn't look at all happy, and he didn't reply at all to the greetings of the others. But when Old Mother Nature spoke to him he was very polite.

"Good morning, Johnny Chuck," said she.

Johnny bobbed his head and said, "Good morning."

"I understand," continued Old Mother Nature, "That you are not at all interested in learning about your relatives. I am sorry for any one who doesn't want to learn. The more one knows the better fitted he is to take care of himself and do his part in the work of the Great World. However, it wasn't for your benefit that I sent word for you to be here this morning. It was for the benefit of your friends and neighbors. Now sit up so that all can get a good look at you."

Johnny Chuck obediently sat up, and of course all the others stared at him. It made him feel quite uncomfortable. "You remember," said Old Mother Nature, "how surprised you little folks were when I told you that Johnny Chuck is a member of the Squirrel family. Happy Jack, you go sit beside Johnny Chuck, and the rest of you look hard at Happy Jack and Johnny and see if you do not see a family resemblance."

Seeing Happy Jack and Johnny Chuck sitting up side by side, Peter Rabbit caught the resemblance at once. There was sort of family look about them. "Why! Why-ee! Johnny Chuck does look like a Squirrel," he exclaimed.

"Of course he looks like a Squirrel, because he is one," said Old Mother Nature. "Johnny Chuck is very much bigger and so stout in the body that he has none of the gracefulness of the true Squirrels. But you will notice that the shape of his head is much the same as that of Happy Jack. He has a Squirrel face when you come to look at him closely. The Woodchucks, sometimes called Ground Hogs, though why any one should call them this is more than I can understand, belong to the Marmot branch of the Squirrel family, and wherever found they look much alike.

"As you will notice, Johnny Chuck's coat is brownish-yellow, his feet are very dark brown, almost black. His head is dark brown with light gray on his cheeks. Beneath he is reddish-orange, including his throat. His tail is short for a member of the Squirrel family, and although it is bushy, it is not very big. He has a number of whiskers and they are black. Some Woodchucks are quite gray, and occasionally there is one who is almost, or wholly black, just as there are black Gray Squirrels.

"Johnny, here, is not fond of the Green Forest, but loves the Old orchard and the Green Meadows. In some parts of the country there are members of his family who prefer to live just on the edge of the Green Forest. You will notice that Johnny has stout claws. Those are to help him dig, for all the Marmot family are great diggers. What other use do you have for those claws, Johnny?"

"They help me to climb," replied Johnny promptly.

"Climb!" exclaimed Peter Rabbit. "Who ever heard of a Woodchuck climbing?"

"I can climb if I have to," retorted Johnny Chuck

indignantly. "I've climbed up bushes and low trees lots of times, and if I can get a good run first, I can climb up the straight trunk of a tree with rough bark to the first branches —if they are not too far above ground. You ask Reddy Fox if I can't; he knows."

"That's quite true, Johnny," said Old Mother Nature. "You can climb a little, but as a real climber you are not much of a success. You are better as a digger."

"He certainly is all right as a digger," exclaimed Peter Rabbit. "My, how he can make the sand fly! Johnny Chuck certainly is right at home when it comes to digging."

"You ought to be thankful that he is," said Old Mother Nature, "for the holes he has dug have saved your life more than once. By the way, Peter, since you are so well acquainted with those holes, suppose you tell us what kind of a home Johnny Chuck has."

Peter was delighted to air his knowledge. "The last one I was in," said he, "was a long tunnel slanting down for quite a distance and then straightening out. The entrance was quite large with a big heap of sand out in front of it. Down a little way the tunnel grew smaller and then remained the same size all the rest of the way. Way down at the farther end was a nice little bedroom with some grass in it. There were one or two other little rooms, and there were two branch tunnels leading up to the surface of the ground, making side or back doorways. There was no sand around either of these, and they were quite hidden by the long grass hanging over them. I don't understand how Johnny made those doorways without leaving any sand on the doorsteps."

"Huh!" interrupted Johnny Chuck. "That was easy enough. I pushed all the sand out of the main doorway so that there would be nothing to attract the attention of any one passing near those back doorways. Those back doorways are very handy in time of danger."

"Do you always have three doorways?" asked Happy Jack.

"No," replied Johnny Chuck. "Sometimes I have only

two and once in a while only one. But that isn't really safe, and I mean always to have at least two."

"Do you use the same house year after year?" piped up Striped Chipmunk.

Johnny shook his head. "No," said he. "I dig a new hole each spring. Mrs. Chuck and I like a change of scene. Usually my new home isn't very far from my old one, because I am not fond of traveling. Sometimes, however, if we cannot find a place that just suits us, we go quite a distance."

"Are your babies born down in that little bedroom in the ground?" asked Jumper the Hare.

"Of course," replied Johnny Chuck. "Where else would they be born?"

"I didn't know but Mrs. Chuck might make a nest on the ground the way Mrs. Peter and Mrs. Jumper do," replied Jumper meekly.

"No, siree!" replied Johnny. "Our babies are born in that little underground bedroom, and they stay down in the ground until they are big enough to hunt for food for themselves."

"How many do you usually have?" inquired Chatterer the Red Squirrel.

"Six or eight," replied Johnny Chuck. "Mrs. Chuck and I believe in large families."

"Do you eat nuts like the rest of our family?" inquired Striped Chipmunk.

"No," replied Johnny Chuck. "Give me green food every time. There is nothing so good as tender sweet clover and young grass, unless it be some of those fine vegetables Farmer Brown grows in his garden."

Peter Rabbit nodded his head very emphatically as if he quite agreed.

"I suppose you are what is called a vegetarian, then," said Happy Jack, to which Johnny Chuck replied that he supposed he was. "And I suppose that is why you sleep all winter," added Happy Jack.

"If I didn't I would starve," responded Johnny Chuck

JOHNNY CHUCK. The familiar Woodchuck is a true Marmot.

WHISTLER THE HOARY MARMOT. The largest of the Marmots. He lives high up on the mountains of the West.

promptly. "When it gets near time for Jack Frost to arrive, I stuff and stuff and stuff on the last of the good green things until I'm so fat I can hardly waddle. Then I go down to my bedroom, curl up and go to sleep. Cold weather, snow and ice don't worry me a bit."

"I know," spoke up Striped Chipmunk. "I sleep most of the winter myself. Of course I have a lot of food stored away down in my house, and once in a while I wake up and eat a little. Do you ever wake up in the winter, Johnny Chuck?"

"No," replied Johnny. "I sleep right through, thank goodness. Sometimes I wake up very early in the spring before the snow is all gone, earlier than I wish I did. That is where my fat comes in handy. It keeps me warm and keeps me alive until I can find the first green plants. Perhaps you have noticed that early in the spring I am as thin as I was fat in the fall. This is because I have used up the fat, waiting for the first green things to appear."

"Do you have many enemies?" asked Peter Rabbit, who has so many himself that he is constantly thinking of them.

"Not many, but enough," growled Johnny Chuck. "Reddy Fox, Old Man Coyote, men and Dogs are the worst. Of course, when I was small I always had to be watching out for Hawks, and of course, like all the rest of us little folks, I am afraid of Shadow the Weasel. Reddy Fox has tried to dig me out more than once, but I can dig faster than he can. If he ever gets me cornered, he'll find that I can fight. A small Dog surprised me once before I could get to my hole and I guess that Dog never will tackle another Woodchuck."

"Time is up," interrupted Old Mother Nature. "Johnny Chuck has a big cousin out in the mountains of the Great West named Whistler, and on the prairies of the Great West he has a smaller cousin named Yap Yap. They are quite important members of the Marmot family, and tomorrow I'll tell you about them if you want me to. You need not come tomorrow, Johnny Chuck, unless you want to," she added.

Johnny Chuck hung his head, for he was a little ashamed

that he had been so unwilling to come that morning.

"If you please, Mother Nature," said he, "I think I'll come. I didn't know I had any close relatives, and I want to know about them."

So it was agreed that all would be on hand at sun-up the next morning, and then everybody started for home to think over the things they had learned.

CHAPTER VIII
WHISTLER AND YAP YAP

Johnny Chuck was the first one on hand the next morning. The fact is, Johnny was quite excited over the discovery that he had some near relatives. He always had supposed that the Woodchucks were a family by themselves. Now that he knew that he had some close relatives, he was filled with quite as much curiosity as ever Peter Rabbit possessed. Just as soon as Old Mother Nature was ready to begin, Johnny Chuck was ready with a question. "If you please," said he, "who are my nearest relatives?"

"The Marmots of the Far West," replied Old Mother Nature. "You know, you are a Marmot, and these cousins of yours out there are a great deal like you in a general way. The biggest and handsomest of all is Whistler, who lives in the mountains of the Northwest. The fact is, he is the biggest of all the Marmot family."

"Is he much bigger than Johnny Chuck?" asked Peter Rabbit.

"Considerably bigger," replied Old Mother Nature, nodding her head. "Considerably bigger. I should think he would weigh twice as much as Johnny."

Johnny's eyes opened very wide. "My!" he exclaimed, "I should like to see him. Does he look like me?"

"In his shape he does," said Old Mother Nature, "but he has a very much handsomer coat. His coat is a mixture of dark brown and white hairs which give him a grayish color. The upper part of his head, his feet and nails are black, and so are his ears. A black band runs from behind each ear down to his neck. His chin is pure white and there is white on his nose. Underneath he is a light, rusty color. His fur is thicker and softer than yours, Johnny; this is because he lives where it is colder. His tail is larger, somewhat bushier, and is a blackish-brown."

"If you please, why is he called Whistler?" asked Johnny Chuck eagerly.

"Because he has a sharp, clear whistle which can be heard a very long distance," replied Old Mother Nature. "He sits up just as you do. If he sees danger approaching he whistles, as a warning to all his relatives within hearing."

"I suppose it is foolish to ask if he lives in a hole in the ground as Johnny Chuck does," spoke up Peter Rabbit.

"He does," replied Old Mother Nature. "All Marmots live in holes in the ground, but Whistler lives in entirely different country. He lives up on the sides of the mountains, often so high that no trees grow there and the ground is rocky. He digs his hole down in between the rocks."

"It must be a nice, safe hole," said Peter. "I guess he doesn't have to worry about being dug out by Reddy fox."

"You guessed quite right," laughed Old Mother Nature. "Nevertheless, he has reason to fear being dug out. You see, out where he lives, Grizzly, the big cousin of Buster Bear, also lives, and Grizzly is very fond of a Marmot dinner when he can get one. He is so big and strong and has such great claws that he can pull the rocks apart and dig Whistler out. By the way, I forgot to tell you that Whistler is also called the Gray Marmot and the Hoary Marmot. He lives on grass and other green things and, like Johnny Chuck, gets very fat in the fall and then sleeps all winter. There are one or two other Marmots in the Far West who live farther south than does Whistler, but their habits are much the same as those of Whistler and Johnny Chuck. None of them are social. I mean by that you never find two Marmot homes very close together. In this they differ from Johnny's smaller cousin, Yap Yap the Prairie Dog. Yap Yap wouldn't be happy if he didn't have close neighbors of his own kind. He has one of the most social natures of all my little people."

"Tell us about him," begged Happy Jack Squirrel before Johnny Chuck, who is naturally slow, could ask for the same thing.

"Yap Yap is the smallest of the Marmot family," said Old Mother Nature. "In a way he is about as closely related to the Ground Squirrels as he is to the Marmots. Johnny Chuck has only four claws on each front foot, but Yap Yap has five, just as the Ground Squirrels have. He looks very much like a small Chuck dressed in light yellow-brown. His tail for the most part is the same color as his coat, but the end is black, though there is one member of the family whose tail has a white tip. In each cheek is a small pouch, that is, a small pocket, and this is one of the things that shows how closely related to the Spermophiles he is.

"As I said before, Yap Yap is very social by nature. He lives on the great open plains of the West and Southwest, frequently where it is very dry and rain seldom falls. When you find his home you are sure to find the homes of many more Prairie Dogs very close at hand. Sometimes there are hundreds and hundreds of homes, making a regular town. This is because the Prairie Dogs dearly love the company of their own kind."

"Does Yap Yap dig the same kind of a hole that I do?" asked Johnny Chuck.

"In a way it is like yours," replied Old Mother Nature, "but at the same time it is different. In the first place, it goes almost straight down for a long distance. In the second place there is no mound of sand in front of Yap Yap's doorway. Instead of that the doorway is right in the very middle of the mound of sand. One reason for this is that when it does rain out where Yap Yap lives it rains very hard indeed, so that the water stands on the ground for a short time. The ground being flat, a lot of water would run down into Yap Yap's home and make him most uncomfortable if he did not do something to keep it out. So he brings the sand out and piles it all the way around his doorway and presses it down with his nose. In that way he builds up a firm mound which he uses for two purposes; one is to keep the water from running down the hole, and the other is as a sort of watch tower. He sits on the top of his mound to watch for his enemies. His cousins with the white tail digs a hole more like yours.

"Yap Yap loves to visit his neighbors and to have them

visit him. They are lively little people and do a great deal of talking among themselves. The instant one of them sees an enemy he gives a signal. Then every Prairie Dog scampers for his own hole and dives in head first. Almost at once he pops his head out again to see what the danger may be."

"How can he do that without going clear to the bottom to turn around?" demanded Peter.

"I wondered if any of you would think of that question," chuckled Old Mother Nature. "Just a little way down from the entrance Yap Yap digs a little room at one side of his tunnel. All he has to do is to scramble into that, turn around and then pop his head out. As I said before, his tunnel goes down very deep; then it turns and goes almost equally far underground. Down there he has a nice little bedroom. Sometimes he has more than one."

"If it is so dry out where he lives, how does he get water to drink?" asked Happy Jack.

"He doesn't have to drink," replied Old Mother Nature. "Some folks think that he digs down until he finds water way down underneath, but this isn't so. He doesn't have to have water. He gets all the moisture he needs from the green things he eats."

"I suppose, like the rest of us, he has lots of enemies?" said Peter.

Old Mother Nature nodded. "Of course," said she. "Old Man Coyote and Reddy Fox are very fond of Prairie Dog. So are members of the Hawk family. Then in some places there is a cousin of Shadow the Weasel called the Black-footed Ferret. He is to be feared most of all because he can follow Yap Yap down into his hole. There is a cousin of Hooty the Owl called the Burrowing Owl because it builds its home in a hole in the ground. You are likely to find many Burrowing Owls living in Prairie Dog villages. Also you are apt to find Buzztail the Rattlesnake there.

"A lot of people believe that Yap Yap, Buzztail and the little Burrowing Owl are the best of friends and often live together in the same hole. This isn't so at all. Buzztail is very fond of young Prairie Dog and so is the Burrowing

YAP YAP THE PRARIE DOG. A social little Marmot who lives on the praries of the West.

GRUBBY THE POCKET GOPHER. The true Gopher and a great pest to farmers.

Owl. Rather than dig a hole for himself the Owl will sometimes take possession of one of Yap Yap's deserted holes. If he should make a mistake and enter a hole in which Yap Yap was at home, the chances are that Yap Yap would kill the Owl for he knows that the Owl is an enemy. Buzztail the Rattlesnake also makes use of Prairie Dog holes, but it is safe to say that if there are any Prairie Dog babies down there they never live to see what the outside world is like. So Buzztail and the Burrowing Owl are really enemies instead of friends of Yap Yap, the Prairie Dog."

"Why is he called a Dog?" asked Peter.

Old Mother Nature laughed right out. "Goodness knows," said she. "He doesn't look like a Dog and he doesn't act like a Dog, so why people should call him a Dog I don't know, unless it is because of his habit of barking, and even his bark isn't at all like a Dog's—not nearly so much so as the bark of Reddy Fox. Now I guess this will do for to-day. Haven't you little folks had enough of school?"

"No," cried Peter Rabbit and Jumper the Hare and Happy Jack and Chatterer the Red Squirrel and Striped Chipmunk and Johnny Chuck. "We want to know about the rest of the members of the order of Rodents or Gnawers," added Peter. "Of course in a way they are sort of related to us and we want to know about them."

Old Mother Nature laughed good-naturedly. "All right," said she, "come again to-morrow morning and we'll see what more we can learn."

CHAPTER IX
Two Queer Little Haymakers

There is nothing like a little knowledge to make one want more. Johnny Chuck, who had gone to school only because Old Mother Nature had sent for him, had become as full of curiosity as Peter Rabbit. The discovery that he had a big, handsome cousin, Whistler the Marmot, living in the mountains of the Far West, had given Johnny something to think about. It seemed to Johnny such a queer place for a member of his family to live that he wanted to know more about it. So Johnny had a question all ready when Old Mother Nature called school to order the next morning.

"If you please, Mother Nature," said he, "does my cousin, Whistler, have any neighbors up among those rocks where he lives?"

"He certainly does," replied Old Mother Nature, nodding her head. "He has for a near neighbor one of the quaintest and most interesting little members of the big order to which you all belong. And that order is what?" she asked abruptly.

"The order of Rodents," replied Peter Rabbit promptly.

"Right, Peter," replied Old Mother Nature, smiling at Peter. "I asked that just to see if you really are learning. I wanted to make sure that I am not wasting my time with you little folks. Now this little neighbor of Whistler is Little Chief Hare."

Instantly Peter Rabbit and Jumper the Hare pricked up their long ears and became more interested than ever, if that were possible. "I thought you had told us all about our family," cried Jumper, "but you didn't mention Little Chief."

"No," said Old Mother Nature, "I didn't, and the reason I didn't was because Little Chief isn't a member of your family. He is called Little Chief Hare, but he isn't a Hare at all, although he looks much like a small Rabbit with short hind legs and rounded ears. He has a family all to himself and should be called a Pika. Some folks do call him that, but more call him a Cony, and some call him the Crying Hare. This is because he uses his voice a great deal, which is something no member of the Hare family does. In size he is just about as big as one of your half-grown babies, Peter, so, you see, he really is a very little fellow. His coat is grayish-brown. His ears are of good size, but instead of being long, are round. He has small bright eyes. His legs are short, his hind legs being very little longer than his front ones. He has hair on the soles of his feet just like the members of the hare family."

"What about his tail?" piped up Peter Rabbit. You know Peter is very much interested in tails.

Old Mother Nature smiled. "He is worse off than you, Peter," said she, "for he hasn't any at all. That is, he hasn't any that can be seen. He lives way up among the rocks of the great mountains above where the trees grow and often is a very near neighbor to Whistler."

"I suppose that means that he makes his home down in under rocks, the same as Whistler does," spoke up Johnny Chuck.

"Right," replied Old Mother Nature. "He is such a little fellow that he can get through very narrow places, and he has his home and barns way down in among the rocks."

"Barns!" exclaimed Happy Jack Squirrel. "Barns! What do you mean by barns?"

Old Mother Nature laughed. "I just call them barns," said she, "because they are the places where he stores away his hay, just as Farmer Brown stores away his hay in his barn. I suppose you would call them storehouses."

At the mention of hay, Peter Rabbit sat bolt upright and his eyes were wide open with astonishment. "Did you say hay?" he exclaimed. "Where under the sun does he get hay way up there, and what does he want of it?"

There was a twinkle in Old Mother Nature's eyes as she replied, "He makes that hay just as you see Farmer Brown make hay every summer. It is what he lives on in the winter and in bad weather. Little Chief knows just as much about the proper way of making hay as Farmer Brown does. Even way up among the rocks there are places where grass and peas-vines and other green things grow. Little Chief lives on these in summer. But he is as wise and thrifty as any Squirrel, another way in which he differs from the Hare family. He cuts them when they are ready for cutting and spreads them out on the rocks to dry in the sun. He knows that if he should take them down into his barns while they are fresh and green they would sour and spoil; so he never stores them away until they are thoroughly dry. Then, of course, they are hay, for hay is nothing but sun-dried grass cut before it has begun to die. When his hay is just as dry as it should be, he takes it down and stores it away in his barns, which are nothing but little caves down in among the rocks. There he has it for use in winter when there is no green food.

"Little Chief is so nearly the color of the rocks that it takes sharp eyes to see him when he is sitting still. He has a funny little squeaking voice, and he uses it a great deal. It is a funny voice because it is hard to tell just where it comes from. It seems to come from nowhere in particular. Sometimes he can be heard squeaking way down in his home under the rocks. Like Johnny Chuck, he prefers to sleep at night and be abroad during the day. Because he is so small he must always be on the lookout for enemies. At the first hint of danger he scampers to safety in among the rocks, and there he scolds whoever has frightened him. There is no more loveable little person in all my great family than this little haymaker of the mountains of the Great West."

"That haymaking is a pretty good idea of Little Chief's," remarked Peter Rabbit, scratching a long ear with a long hind foot. "I've a great mind to try it myself."

Everybody laughed right out, for everybody knew just how easy-going and thriftless Peter was. Peter himself grinned. He couldn't help it.

"That would be a very good idea, Peter," said Old Mother Nature. "By the way, there is another haymaker out in those same great mountains of the Far West."

"Who?" demanded Peter and Johnny Chuck and Happy Jack Squirrel, all in the same breath.

"Stubtail the Mountain Beaver," replied Old Mother Nature.

"I know Paddy the Beaver," declared Peter promptly. "I

suppose Stubtail is his cousin."

Old Mother Nature shook her head. "No," said she. "No. Stubtail and Paddy are no more closely related than the rest of you. Stubtail isn't a Beaver at all. His proper name is Sewellel. Sometimes he is called Showt'l and sometimes the Boomer, and sometimes the Chehalis, but most folks call him the Mountain Beaver."

"Is it because he looks like Paddy the Beaver?" Striped Chipmunk asked.

"No," replied Old Mother Nature. "He looks more like Jerry Muskrat than he does like Paddy. He is about Jerry's size and looks very much as Jerry would if he had no tail."

"Hasn't he any tail at all?" asked Peter.

"Yes, he has a little tail, a little stub of a tail, but it is so small that to look at him you would think he hadn't any," replied Old Mother Nature. "He is found out in the same mountains of the Far West where Whistler and Little Chief live, but instead of living way up high among the rocks he is at home down in the valleys where the ground is soft and the trees grow thickly. Stubtail has no use for rocks. He wants soft, wet ground where he can tunnel and tunnel to his heart's content. In one thing Stubtail is very like Yap Yap the Prairie Dog."

"What is that?" asked Johnny Chuck quickly, for, you know, Yap Yap is Johnny's cousin.

"In his social habits," replied Old Mother Nature. "Stubtail isn't fond of living alone. He wants company of his own kind. So wherever you find Stubtail you are likely to find many of his family. They like to go visiting back and forth. They make little paths between their homes and all about through the thick ferns, and they keep these little paths free and clear, so that they may run along them easily. Some of these little paths lead into long tunnels. These are made for safety. Usually the ground is so wet that there will be water running in the bottoms of these little tunnels."

"What kind of a house does Stubtail have?" inquired Johnny Chuck interestedly.

"A hole in the ground, of course," replied Old Mother Nature. "It is dug where the ground is drier than where the runways are made. Mrs. Stubtail makes a nest of dried ferns and close by they build two or three storehouses, for Stubtail and Mrs. Stubtail are thrifty people."

"I suppose he fills them with hay, for you said he is a haymaker," remarked Happy Jack Squirrel, who is always interested in storehouses.

"Yes," replied Old Mother Nature, "he puts hay in them. He cuts grasses, ferns, pea-vines and other green plants and carries them in little bundles to the entrance to his tunnel. There he piles them on sticks so as to keep them off the damp ground and so that the air can help dry them out. When they are dry, he takes them inside and stores them away. He also stores other things. He likes the roots of ferns. He cuts tender, young twigs from bushes and stores away some of these. He is fond of bark. In winter he is quite as active as in summer and tunnels about under the snow. Then he sometimes has Peter Rabbit's bad habit of killing trees by gnawing bark all around as high up as he can reach."

"Can he climb trees?" asked Chatterer the Red Squirrel.

"Just about as much as Johnny Chuck can," replied Old Mother Nature. "Sometimes he climbs up in low bushes or in small, low-branching trees to cut off tender shoots, but he doesn't do much of this sort of thing. His home is the ground. He is most active at night, but where undisturbed, is out more or less during the day. When he wants to cut off a twig he sits up like a Squirrel and holds the twig in his hands while he bites it off with his sharp teeth."

"You didn't tell us what color his coat is," said Peter Rabbit.

"I told you he looked very much like Jerry Muskrat," replied Old Mother Nature. "His coat is brown, much the color of Jerry's, but his fur is not nearly so soft and fine."

"I suppose he has enemies just as the rest of us little people have," said Peter.

"Of course," replied Old Mother Nature. "All little people have enemies, and most big ones too, for that matter. King Eagle is one and Yowler the Bob Cat is another. They are always watching for Stubtail. That is why he digs so many tunnels. He can travel under the ground then. My goodness, how time flies! Scamper home, all of you, for I have too much to do to talk any more to-day."

LITTLE CHIEF THE PIKA. Also called Cony and Little Chief Hare.

STUBTAIL THE MOUNTAIN BEAVER. He is not a Beaver at all but a Sewellel.

CHAPTER X
Prickly Porky and Grubby Gopher

All the way to school the next morning Peter Rabbit wondered who they would learn about that day. He was so busy wondering that he was heedless. Peter is apt to be heedless at times. The result was that as he hopped out of a bramble-tangle just within the edge of the Green Forest, he all but landed in something worse than the worst brambles that ever grew. It was only by a wild side jump that he saved himself. Peter had almost landed among the thousand little spears of Prickly Porky the Porcupine.

"Gracious!" exclaimed Peter.

"Why don't you look where you are going," grunted Prickly Porky. Plainly he was rather peevish. "It wouldn't be my fault if you had a few of my little spears sticking in you this very minute, and it would serve you right." He waddled along a few steps, then began talking again. "I don't see why Old Mother Nature sent for me this morning," he grumbled. "I hate a long walk."

Peter pricked up his long ears. "I know!" he cried. "You're going to school, Prickly Porky. You're a Rodent, and we are going to learn all about you this morning."

"I'm not a Rodent; I'm a Porcupine," grunted Prickly Porky indignantly.

"You're a Rodent just the same. You've got big gnawing teeth, and any one with that kind of teeth is a Rodent," retorted Peter. Then at a sudden thought a funny look passed over his face. "Why, that means that you and I are related in a way," he added.

"Don't believe it," grunted Prickly Porky, still shuffling along. "Don't believe it. Don't want to be related to anybody as heedless as you. What is this school, anyway? Don't want to go to school. Know all I want to know. Know how to get all I want to eat and how to make everybody get out of my way and leave me alone, and that's enough to know." He rattled the thousand little spears hidden in his coat, and Peter shivered at the sound. It was a most unpleasant sound.

"Well, some folks do like to be stupid," snapped Peter and hurried on, lipperty-lipperty-lip, while Prickly Porky slowly shuffled and rattled along behind.

All the others were there when Peter arrived. Prickly Porky wasn't even in sight. Old Mother Nature wasted no time. She has too much to do ever to waste time. She called the school to order at once.

"Yesterday," she began, "I told you about two little haymakers of the high mountains of the Far West. Who were they, Peter Rabbit?"

"Little Chief Hare, called the Pika or Cony, and Stubtail the Mountain Beaver or Sewellel," replied Peter with great promptness.

"Right," said Old Mother Nature. "Now I am going to tell you of one of my little plowmen who also lives in the Far West but prefers the great plains to the high mountains, though he is sometimes found in the latter. He is Grubby the Gopher, a member of the same order the rest of you belong to, but of a family quite his own. He is properly called the Pocket Gopher, and way down in the Southeast, where he is also found, he is called a Salamander, though what for I haven't the least idea."

"Does he have pockets in his cheeks like mine?" asked Striped Chipmunk eagerly.

"He has pockets in his cheeks, and that is why he is called Pocket Gopher," replied Old Mother Nature; "but they are not at all like yours, Striped Chipmunk. Yours are on the inside of your cheeks, but his are on the outside."

"How funny!" exclaimed Striped Chipmunk.

"Your pockets are small compared with those of Grubby," continued Old Mother Nature. "One of his covers almost the whole side of his head back to his short neck, and it is lined with fur, and remember he has two of them. Grubby uses these for carrying food and never for carrying out earth when he is digging a tunnel, as some folks think he does. He stuffs them full with his front feet and empties them by pressing them from the back with his feet. The Gopher family is quite large and the members range in size from the size of Danny Meadow Mouse to that of Robber the Rat, only these bigger members are stouter and heavier than Robber. Some are reddish-brown and some are gray. But whatever his size and wherever he is found, Grubby's habits are the same."

All this time Peter Rabbit had been fidgeting about. It was quite clear that Peter had something on his mind. Now as Old Mother Nature paused, Peter found the chance he had been waiting for. "If you please, why did you call him a plowman?" he asked eagerly.

"I'm coming to that all in due time," replied Old Mother Nature, smiling at Peter's eagerness. "Grubby Gopher spends most of his life underground, very much like Miner the Mole, whom you all know. He can dig tunnels just about as fast. His legs are short, and his front legs and feet are very stout and strong. They are armed with very long, strong claws and it is with these and the help of his big cutting teeth that Grubby digs. He throws the earth under him and then kicks it behind him with his hind feet. When he has quite a pile behind him he turns around, and with his front feet and head pushes it along to a little side tunnel and then up to the surface of the ground. As soon as he has it all out he plugs up the opening and goes back to digging. The loose earth he has pushed out makes little mounds, and he makes one of these mounds every few feet.

"Grubby is a great worker. He is very industrious. Since he is underground, it doesn't make much difference to him whether it be night or day. In summer, during the hottest part of the day, he rests. His eyes are small and weak because he has little use for them, coming out on the surface very seldom and then usually in the dusk. He has a funny little tail without any hair on it; this is very sensitive and serves him as a sort of guide when he runs backward along his tunnel, which he can do quite fast. A funny thing about those long claws on his front feet is that he folds

PRICKLY PORKY THE PORCUPINE. An independent fellow with a thousand little spears in his coat.

them under when he is walking or running. Do any of you know why Farmer Brown plows his garden?"

As she asked this, Old Mother Nature looked from one to another, and each in turn shook his head. "It is to mix the dead vegetable matter thoroughly with the earth so that the roots of the plants may get it easily," explained Old Mother Nature. "By making those tunnels in every direction and bringing up the earth below to the surface, Grubby Gopher does the same thing. That is why I call him my little plowman. He loosens up the hard, packed earth and mixes the vegetable matter with it and so makes it easy for seeds to sprout and plants to grow."

"Then he must be one of the farmer's best friends," spoke up Happy Jack Squirrel.

Old Mother Nature shook her head. "He has been in the past," said she. "He has done a wonderful work in helping make the land fit for farming. But where land is being farmed he is a dreadful pest, I am sorry to say. You see he eats the crops the farmer tries to raise, and the new mounds he is all the time throwing up bury a lot of the young plants, and in the meadows make it very hard to use a mowing machine for cutting hay. Then Grubby gets into young orchards and cuts off all the tender roots of young trees. This kills them. You see he is fond of tender roots, seeds, stems of grass and grain, and is never happier than when he can find a field of potatoes.

"Being such a worker, he has to have a great deal to eat. Then, too, he stores away a great deal for winter, for he doesn't sleep in winter as Johnny Chuck does. He even tunnels about under the snow. Sometimes he fills these little snow tunnels with the earth he brings up from below, and when the snow melts it leaves queer little earth ridges to show where the tunnels were.

"Grubby is very neat in his habits and keeps his home and himself very clean. During the day he leaves one of his mounds open for a little while to let in fresh air. But it is only for a little while. Then he closes it again. He doesn't dare leave it open very long, for fear Shadow the Weasel or a certain big Snake called the Gopher Snake will find it and come in after him. Digger the Badger is the only one of his enemies who can dig fast enough to dig him out, but at night, when he likes to come out for a little air or to cut grain and grass, he must always watch for Hooty the Owl. Old Man Coyote and members of the Hawk family are always looking for him by day, so you see he has plenty of enemies, like the rest of you.

"He got the name Gopher because that comes from a word meaning honeycomb, and Grubby's tunnels go in every direction until the ground is like honeycomb. He isn't a bit social and has rather a mean disposition. He is always ready to fight. On the plains he has done a great deal to make the soil fine and rich, as I have already told you, but on hillsides he does a great deal of harm. The water runs down his tunnels and washes away the soil. Because of this and the damage he does to crops, man is his greatest enemy. But man has furnished him with new and splendid foods easy to get, and so Grubby's family increases faster than it used to, in spite of traps and poison. Hello! See who's here! It is about time."

There was a shuffling and rattling and grunting, and Prickly Porky climbed up on an old stump, looking very peevish and much out of sorts. He had come to school much against his will.

CHAPTER XI
A FELLOW WITH A THOUSAND SPEARS

"There," said Old Mother Nature, pointing to Prickly Porky the Porcupine, "is next to the largest member of your order, which is?"

"Order of Rodents," piped up Striped Chipmunk.

"He is not only next to the largest, but is the stupidest," continued Old Mother Nature. "At least that is what people say of him, though I suspect he isn't as stupid as he sometimes seems. Anyway, he manages to keep well fed and escape his enemies, which is more than can be said for some others who are supposed to have quick wits."

"Escaping his enemies is no credit to him. They are only too glad to keep out of his way; he doesn't have to fear anybody," said Chatterer the Red Squirrel to his cousin, Happy Jack.

His remark didn't escape the keen ears of Old Mother Nature. "Are you sure about that?" she demanded. "Now there's Pekan the Fisher-"

She was interrupted by a great rattling on the old stump. Everybody turned to look. There was Prickly Porky backing down as fast as he could, which wasn't fast at all, and rattling his thousand little spears as he did so. It was really very funny. Everybody had to laugh, even Old Mother Nature. You see, it was plain that he was in a great hurry, yet every movement was slow and clumsy.

"Well, Prickly Porky, what does this mean? Where are you going?" demanded Old Mother Nature.

Prickly Porky turned his dull-looking eyes towards her, and in them was a troubled, worried look. "Where's Pekan the Fisher?" he asked, and his voice shook a little with something very much like fear.

Old Mother Nature understood instantly. When she had said, "Now there's Pekan the Fisher," Prickly Porky had waited to hear no more. He had instantly thought that she meant that Pekan was right there somewhere. "It's all right, Prickly Porky," said she. "Pekan isn't anywhere around here, so climb back on that stump and don't worry. Had you waited for me to finish, you would have saved yourself a fright. Chatterer had just said that you didn't have to fear anybody and I was starting to explain that he was wrong, that despite your thousand little spears you have reason to fear Pekan the Fisher."

Prickly Porky shivered and this made the thousand little spears in his coat rattle. It was such a surprising thing to see Prickly Porky actually afraid that the other little folks almost doubted their own eyes. "Are you quite sure that Pekan isn't anywhere around?" asked Prickly Porky, and his voice still shook.

"Quite sure," replied Old Mother Nature. "If he were I wouldn't allow him to hurt you. You ought to know that. Now sit up so that every one can get a good look at you."

Prickly Porky sat up, and the others gathered around the foot of the stump to look at him. "He certainly is no beauty," murmured Happy Jack Squirrel.

Happy Jack was quite right. He was anything but handsome. The truth is he was the homeliest, clumsiest-looking fellow in all the Green Forest. He was a little bigger than Bobby Coon and his body was thick and heavy-looking. His back humped up like an arch. His head was rather small for the size of his body, short and rather round. His neck was even shorter. His eyes were small and very dull. It was plain that he couldn't see far, or clearly unless what he was looking at was close at hand. His ears were small and nearly hidden in hair. His front teeth, the gnawing teeth which showed him to be a Rodent, were very large and bright orange. His legs were short and stout. He had four toes on each front foot and five on each hind foot, and these were armed with quite long, stout claws.

But the queerest thing and the most interesting thing

about Prickly Porky was his coat. Not one among the other little people of the Green Forest has a coat anything like his. Most of them have a soft, short under fur protected and more or less hidden by longer, coarser hair. Prickly Porky had the long coarse hair and on his back it was very long and coarse, brownish-black in color up to the tips, which were white. Under this long hair was some soft woolly fur, but what that long hair hid chiefly was an array of wicked-looking little spears called quills. They were white to the tips, which were dark and very, very sharply pointed. All down the sides were tiny barbs, so small as hardly to be seen, but there just the same. On his head the quills were about an inch long, but on his back they were four inches long, becoming shorter towards the tail. The latter was rather short, stout, and covered with short quills.

As he sat there on that old stump some of Prickly Porky's little spears could be seen peeping out from the long hair on his back, but they didn't look particularly dangerous. Peter Rabbit suddenly made a discovery. "Why!" he exclaimed. "He hasn't any little spears on the under side of him!"

"I wondered who would be the first to notice that," said Old Mother Nature. "No, Prickly Porky hasn't any little spears underneath, and Pekan the Fisher has found that out. He knows that if he can turn Prickly Porky on his back he can kill him without much danger from those little spears, and he has learned how to do that very thing. That is why Prickly Porky is afraid of him. Now, Prickly Porky, climb down off that stump and show these little folks what you do when an enemy comes near."

Grumbling and growling, Prickly Porky climbed down to the ground. Then he tucked his head down between his front paws and suddenly the thousand little spears appeared all over him, pointing in every direction until he looked like a giant chestnut burr. Then he began to thrash his tail from side to side.

"What is he doing that for?" asked Johnny Chuck, looking rather puzzled.

"Go near enough to be hit by it, and you'll understand," said Old Mother Nature dryly. "That is his one weapon. Whoever is hit by that tail will find himself full of those little spears and will take care never to go near Prickly Porky again. Once those little spears have entered the skin, they keep working in deeper and deeper, and more than one of his enemies has been killed by them. On account of those tiny barbs they are hard to pull out, and pulling them out hurts dreadfully. Just try one and see."

But no one was anxious to try, so Old Mother Nature paused only a moment. "You will notice that he moves that tail quickly," she continued. "It is the only thing about him which is quick. When he has a chance, in time of danger, he likes to get his head under a log or rock, instead of putting it between his paws as he is doing now. Then he plants his feet firmly and waits for a chance to use that tail."

"Is it true that he can throw those little spears at folks?" asked Peter.

Old Mother Nature shook her head. "There isn't a word of truth in it," she declared. "That story probably was started by some one who was hit by his tail, and it was done so quickly that the victim didn't see the tail move and so thought the little spears were thrown at him."

"How does he make all those little spears stand up that way?" asked Jumper the Hare.

"He has a special set of muscles for just that purpose," explained Old Mother Nature.

"When those quills stick into some one they must pull out of Prickly Porky's own skin; I should think that would hurt him," spoke up Striped Chipmunk.

"Not at all," replied Old Mother Nature. "They are very loosely fastened in his skin and come out at the least little pull. New Ones grow to take the place of those he loses. Notice that he puts his whole foot flat on the ground just as Buster Bear and Bobby Coon do, and just as those two-legged creatures called men do. Very few animals do this, and those that do are said to be plantigrade. Now, Prickly Porky, tell us what you eat and where you make your home, and that will end today's lesson."

"I eat bark, twigs and leaves mostly," grunted Prickly Porky ungraciously. "I like hemlock best of all, but also eat poplar, pine and other trees for a change. Sometimes I stay in a tree for days until I have stripped it of all its bark and leaves. I don't see any sense in moving about any more than is necessary."

"But that must kill the tree!" exclaimed Peter Rabbit.

"Well, what of it?" demanded Prickly Porky crossly. "There are plenty of trees. In summer I like lily pads and always get them when I can."

"Can you swim?" asked Peter eagerly.

"Of course," grunted Prickly Porky.

"I never see you out on the Green Meadows," said Peter.

"And you never will," retorted Prickly Porky. "The Green Forest for me every time. Summer or winter, I'm at home there."

"Don't you sleep through the cold weather the way Buster Bear and I do?" asked Johnny Chuck.

"What should I sleep for?" grumbled Prickly Porky. "Cold weather doesn't bother me. I like it. I have the Green Forest pretty much to myself then. I like to be alone. And as long as there are trees, there is plenty to eat. I sleep a great deal in the daytime because I like night best."

"What about your home?" asked Happy Jack.

"Home is wherever I happen to be, most of the time, but Mrs. Porky has a home in a hollow log or a cave or under the roots of a tree where the babies are born. I guess that's all I've got to tell you."

"You might add that those babies are big for the size of their mother and have a full supply of quills when they are born," said Old Mother Nature. "And you forgot to say how fond of salt you are, and how often this fondness gets you into trouble around the camps of men. Your fear of Pekan the Fisher we all saw. I might add that Puma the Panther is to be feared at times, and when he is very hungry Buster Bear will take a chance on turning you on your back. By the way, don't any of you call Prickly Porky a Hedgehog. He isn't any thing of the kind. He is sometimes called a Quill Pig, but his real name, Porcupine, is best. He has no near relatives. Tomorrow morning, instead of meeting here, we'll hold school on the shore of the pond Paddy the Beaver has made. School is dismissed."

PADDY THE BEAVER. This shows his wonderful dam and his house.

CHAPTER XII
A LUMBERMAN AND ENGINEER

Johnny Chuck and Striped Chipmunk were the only ones who were not on hand at the pond of Paddy the Beaver deep in the Green Forest at sun-up the next morning. Johnny and Striped Chipmunk were afraid to go so far from home. To the surprise of everybody, Prickly Porky was there.

"He must have traveled all night to get here he is such a slow-poke," said Peter Rabbit to his cousin, Jumper the Hare.

Peter wasn't far from the truth. But how ever he got there, there he was, reaching for lily pads from an old log which lay half in the water, and appearing very well satisfied with life. You know there is nothing like a good meal of things you like, to make everything seem just as it should.

Old Mother Nature seated herself on one end of Paddy's dam and called the school to order. Just as she did so a brown head popped out of the water close by and a pair of anxious eyes looked up at Old Mother Nature.

"It is quite all right, Paddy," said she softly. "These little folks are trying to gain a little knowledge of themselves and other folks, and we are going to have this morning's lesson right here because it is to be about you."

Paddy the Beaver no longer looked anxious. There was a sparkle in his eyes. "May I stay?" he asked eagerly. "If there is a chance to learn anything I don't want to miss it."

Before Old Mother Nature could reply Peter Rabbit spoke up. "But the lesson is to be about you and your family. Do you expect to learn anything about yourself?" he demanded, and chuckled as if he thought that a great joke.

"It seems to me that some one named Peter learned a great deal about his own family when he first came to school to me," said Old Mother Nature. Peter had grace enough to hang his head and look ashamed. "Of course you may stay, Paddy. In fact, I want you to. There are some things I shall want you to explain. That is why we are holding school over here this morning. Just come up here on your dam where we can all get a good look at you."

Paddy the Beaver climbed out on his dam. It was the first time Happy Jack Squirrel ever had seen him out of water, and Happy Jack gave a little gasp of surprise. "I had no idea he is so big!" he exclaimed.

"He is the biggest of all the Rodents in this country, and one of the biggest in all the Great World. Also he is the smartest member of the whole order," said Old Mother Nature.

"He doesn't look it," said Chatterer the Squirrel with a saucy jerk of his tail.

"Which means, I suppose, that you haven't the least doubt that you are quite as smart as he," said Old Mother Nature quietly, and Chatterer looked both guilty and a little bit ashamed. "I'll admit that you are smart, Chatterer, but often it is in a wrong way. Paddy is smart in the very best way. He is a lumberman, builder and engineer. A lot of my little people are workers, but they are destructive workers. The busier they are, the more they destroy. Paddy the Beaver is a constructive worker. That means that he is a builder instead of a destroyer."

"How about all those trees he cuts down? If that isn't destroying, I don't know what is!" said Chatterer, and with each word jerked his tail as if somehow his tongue and tail were connected.

"So it is," replied Old Mother Nature good-naturedly. "But just think of the number of trees you destroy."

"I never have destroyed a tree in my life!" declared Chatterer indignantly.

"Yes, you have," retorted Old Mother Nature.

"I never have!" contradicted Chatterer, quite forgetting to whom he was speaking.

But Old Mother Nature overlooked this. "I don't

suppose you ever ate a chestnut or a fat hickory nut or a sweet beechnut," said she softly.

"Of course," retorted Chatterer sharply. "I've eaten ever and ever and ever so many of them. What of it?"

"In the heart of each one was a little tree," explained Old Mother Nature. "But for you very many of those little trees would have sprung up and some day would have made big trees. So you see for every tree Paddy has destroyed you probably have destroyed a hundred. You eat the nuts that you may live. Paddy cuts down the trees that he may live, for the bark of those trees is his food. Like Prickly Porky he lives chiefly on bark. But, unlike Prickly Porky, he doesn't destroy a tree for the bark alone. He wastes nothing. He makes use of every bit of that tree. He does something for the Green Forest in return for the trees he takes."

Chatterer looked at Happy Jack and blinked in a puzzled way. Happy Jack looked at Peter Rabbit and blinked. Peter looked at Jumper the Hare and blinked. Jumper looked at Prickly Porky and blinked. Then all looked at Paddy the Beaver and finally at Old Mother Nature, and all blinked. Old Mother Nature chuckled.

"Don't you think the Green Forest is more beautiful because of this little pond?" she asked. Everybody nodded. "Of course," she continued. "But there wouldn't be any little pond here were it not for Paddy and the trees he has cut. He destroyed the trees in order to make the pond. That is what I meant when I called him a constructive worker. Now I want you all to take a good look at Paddy. Then he will show us just how as a lumberman he cuts trees, as a builder he constructs houses and dams, and as an engineer he digs canals."

As Paddy sat there on his dam, he looked rather like a giant member of the Rat family, though his head was more like that of a Squirrel than a Rat. His body was very thick and heavy, and in color he was dark brown, lighter underneath than above. Squatting there on the dam his back was rounded. All together, he was a very clumsy-looking fellow.

Peter Rabbit appeared to be interested in just one thing, Paddy's tail. He couldn't keep his eyes off it.

Old Mother Nature noticed this. "Well, Peter," said she, "what have you on your mind now?"

"That tail," replied Peter. "That's the queerest tail I've ever seen. I should think it would be heavy and dreadfully in the way."

Old Mother Nature laughed. "If you ask him Paddy will tell you that that tail is the handiest tail in the Green Forest," said she. "There isn't another like it in all the Great World, and if you'll be patient you will see just how handy it is."

It was a queer-looking tail. It was broad and thick and flat, oval in shape, and covered with scales instead of hair. Just then Jumper the Hare made a discovery. "Why!" he exclaimed, "Paddy has feet like Honker the Goose!"

"Only my hind feet," said Paddy. "They have webs between the toes just as Honker's have. That is for swimming. But there are no webs between my fingers." He held up a hand for all to see. Sure enough, the fingers were free.

"Now that everybody has had a good look at you, Paddy," said Old Mother Nature, "suppose you swim over to where you have been cutting trees. We will join you there, and then you can show us just how you work."

Paddy slipped into the water, where for a second or two he floated with just his head above the surface. Then he quickly raised his broad, heavy tail and brought it down on the water with a slap that sounded like the crack of a terrible gun. It was so loud and unexpected that every one save Old Mother Nature and Prickly Porky jumped with fright. Peter Rabbit happened to be right on the edge of the dam and, because he jumped before he had time to think, he jumped right into the water with a splash. Now Peter doesn't like the water, as you know, and he scrambled out just as fast as ever he could. How the others did laugh at him.

"What did he do that for?" demanded Peter indignantly.

"To show you one use he has for that handy tail," replied Old Mother Nature. "That is the way he gives warning to his friends whenever he discovers danger. Did you notice how he used his tail to aid him in swimming? He turns it almost on edge and uses it as a rudder. Those big, webbed hind feet are the paddles which drive him through the water. He can stay under water a long time—as much as five minutes. See, he has just come up now."

Sure enough, Paddy's head had just appeared clear across the pond almost to the opposite shore, and he was now swimming on the surface. Old Mother Nature at once led the way around the pond to a small grove of poplar trees which stood a little way back from the water. Paddy was already there. "Now," said Old Mother Nature "show us what kind of a lumberman you are."

Paddy picked out a small tree, sat up much as Happy Jack Squirrel does, but with his big flat tail on the ground to brace him, seized the trunk of the tree in both hands, and went to work with his great orange-colored cutting teeth. He bit out a big chip. Then another and another. Gradually he worked around the tree. After a while the tree began to sway and crack. Paddy bit out two or three more chips, then suddenly slapped the ground with his tail as a warning and scampered back to a safe distance. He was taking no chances of being caught under that falling tree.

The tree fell, and at once Paddy returned to work. The smaller branches he cut off with a single bite at the base of each. The larger ones required a number of bites. Then he set to work to cut the trunk up in short logs. At this point Old Mother Nature interrupted.

"Now show us," said she, "what you do with the logs."

Paddy at once got behind a log, and by pushing, rolled it ahead of him until at last it fell with a splash in the water of a ditch or canal which led from near that grove of trees to the pond. Paddy followed into the water and began to push it ahead of him towards the pond.

"That will do," spoke up Old Mother Nature. "Come out and show us how you take the branches."

Obediently Paddy climbed out and returned to the fallen tree. There he picked up one of the long branches in his mouth, grasping it near the butt, twisted it over his shoulder and started to drag it to the canal. When he reached the latter he entered the water and began swimming, still dragging the branch in the same way. Once more Old Mother Nature stopped him. "You've shown us how you cut trees and move them, so now I want you to answer a few questions," said she.

Paddy climbed out and squatted on the bank.

"How did this canal happen to be here handy?" asked Old Mother Nature.

"Why, I dug it, of course," replied Paddy looking surprised. "You see, I'm rather slow and clumsy on land, and don't like to be far from water. Those trees are pretty well back from the pond, so I dug this canal, which brings the water almost to them. It makes it safer for me in case Old Man Coyote or Buster Bear or Yowler the Bobcat happens to be looking for a Beaver dinner. Also it makes it very much easier to get my logs and branches to the pond."

Old Mother Nature nodded. "Just so," said she. "I want the rest of you to notice how well this canal has been dug. At the other end it is carried along the bottom of the pond where the water is shallow so as to give greater depth. Now you will understand why I called Paddy an engineer. What do you do with your logs and branches, Paddy?"

"Put them in my food-pile, out there where the water is deep near my house," replied Paddy promptly. "The bark I eat, and the bare sticks I use to keep my house and dam in repair. In the late fall I cut enough trees to keep me in food all winter. When my pond is covered with ice I have nothing to worry about; my food supply is below the ice. When I am hungry I swim out under the ice, get a stick, take it back into my house and eat the bark. Then I take the bare stick outside to use when needed on my dam or house."

"How did you come to make this fine pond?" asked Old Mother Nature.

"Oh, I just happened to come exploring up the Laughing Brook and found there was plenty of food here and a good place for a pond," replied Paddy. "I thought I would like to live here. Down where my dam is, the Laughing Brook was shallow—just the place for a dam."

"Tell us why you wanted a pond and how you built that dam," commanded Old Mother Nature.

"Why, I had to have a pond, if I was to stay here," replied Paddy, as if every one must understand that. "The Laughing Brook wasn't deep or big enough for me to live here safely. If it had been, I would have made my home in the bank and not bothered with a house or dam. But it wasn't, so I had to make a pond. It required a lot of hard work, but it is worth all it cost.

"First, I cut a lot of brush and young trees and placed them in the Laughing Brook in that shallow place, with the butts pointing up-stream. I kept them in place by piling mud and stones on them. Then I kept piling on more sticks and brush and mud. The water brought down leaves and floating stuff, and this caught in the dam and helped fill it in. I dug a lot of mud in front of it and used this to fill in the spaces between the sticks. This made the water deeper in front of the dam and at the same time kept it from getting through. As the water backed up, of course it made a pond. I kept making my dam longer and higher, and the longer and higher it became the bigger the pond grew. When it was big enough and deep enough to suit me, I stopped work on the dam and built my house out there."

Everybody turned to look at Paddy's house, the roof of which stood high out of water a little way from the dam. "Tell us how you built that," said Old Mother Nature quietly.

"Oh, I just made a big platform of sticks and mud out there where it was deep enough for me to be sure that the water could not freeze clear to the bottom, even in the coldest weather," replied Paddy, in a matter-of-fact tone. "I built it up until it was above water. Then I built the walls and roof of sticks and mud, just as you see them there.

Inside I have a fine big room with a comfortable bed of shredded wood. I have two openings in the floor with a long passage leading from each down through the foundations and opening at the bottom of the pond. Of course, these are filled with water. Some houses have only one passage, but I like two. These are the only entrances to my house.

"Every fall I repair my walls and roof, adding sticks and mud and turf, so that now they are very thick. Late in the fall I sometimes plaster the outside with mud. This freezes hard, and no enemy who may reach my house on the ice can tear it open. I guess that's all."

Peter Rabbit drew a long breath. "What dreadful lot of work," said he. "Do you work all the time?"

Paddy chuckled. "No, Peter," said he. And Old Mother Nature nodded in approval. "Quite right," said she. "Quite right. Are there any more questions?"

"Do you eat nothing but bark?" It was Happy Jack Squirrel who spoke.

"Oh, no," replied Paddy. "In summer I eat berries, mushrooms, grass and the leaves and stems of a number of plants. In winter I vary my fare with lily roots and the roots of alder and willow. But bark is my principal food."

Old Mother Nature waited a few minutes, but as there were no more questions she added a few words. "Now I hope you understand why I am so proud of Paddy the Beaver, and why I told you that he is a lumberman, builder and engineer," said she. "For the next lesson we will take up the Rat family."

CHAPTER XIII
A Worker and a Robber

"Now we come to the largest family of the Rodent order, the Rat family, which of course includes the Mice," said Old Mother Nature, after calling school to order at the old meeting-place. "And the largest member of the family reminds me very much of the one we learned about yesterday."

"I know!" cried Peter Rabbit. "You mean Jerry Muskrat."

"Go to the head of the class, Peter," said Old Mother Nature, smiling. "Jerry is the very one, the largest member of the Rat family. Sometimes he is spoken of as a little cousin of Paddy the Beaver. Probably this is because he looks something like a small Beaver, builds a house in the water as Paddy does, and lives in very much the same way. The truth is, he is no more closely related to Paddy than he is to the rest of you. He is a true Rat. He is called Muskrat because he carries with him a scent called musk. It is not an unpleasant scent, like that of Jimmy Skunk, and isn't used for the same purpose. Jerry uses his to tell his friends where he has been. He leaves a little of it at the places he visits. Some folks call him Musquash, but Muskrat is better.

"Jerry is seldom found far from the water and then only when he is seeking a new home. He is rather slow and awkward on land; but in the water he is quite at home, as all of you know who have visited the Smiling Pool. He can dive and swim under water a long distance, though not as far as Paddy the Beaver."

"Has he webbed hind feet like Paddy?" piped up Jumper the Hare.

"Yes and no," replied Old Mother Nature. "They are not fully webbed as Paddy's are, but there is a little webbing between some of the toes, enough to be of great help in swimming. His tail is of greater use in swimming than is Paddy's. It is bare and scaly, but instead of being flat top and bottom it is flattened on the sides, and he uses it as a propeller, moving it rapidly from side to side.

"Like Paddy he has a dark brown outer coat, lighter underneath than on his back and sides, and like Paddy he has a very warm soft under coat, through which the water cannot get and which keeps him comfortable, no matter how cold the water is. You have all seen his house in the Smiling Pool. He builds it in much the same way that Paddy builds his, but instead of sticks he cuts and uses rushes. Of course it is not nearly as large as Paddy's house, because Jerry is himself so much smaller. It is arranged much the same, with a comfortable bedroom and one or more passages down to deep water. In winter Jerry spends much of his time in this house, going out only for food. Then he lives chiefly on lily roots and roots of other water plants, digging them up and taking them back to his house to eat. When the ice is clear you can sometimes see him swimming below."

"I know," spoke up Peter Rabbit. "Once I was crossing the Smiling Pool on the ice and saw him right under me."

"Jerry doesn't build dams, but he sometimes digs little canals along the bottom where the water isn't deep enough to suit him," continued Old Mother Nature. "Sometimes in the winter Jerry and Mrs. Jerry share their home with two or three friends. If there is a good bank Jerry usually has another home in that. He makes the entrance under water and then tunnels back and up for some distance, where he builds a snug little bedroom just below the surface of the ground where it is dry. Usually he has more than one tunnel leading to this, and sometimes an opening from above. This is covered with sticks and grass to hide it, and provides an entrance for fresh air.

"Jerry lives mostly on roots and plants, but is fond of mussels or fresh-water clams, fish, some insects and, I am sorry to say, young birds when he can catch them. Jerry could explain where some of the babies of Mr. and Mrs. Quack the Ducks have disappeared to. Paddy the Beaver doesn't eat flesh at all.

JERRY MUSKRAT. He is the largest of American Rats. Note how his tail is flattened.

"Jerry and Mrs. Jerry have several families in a year, and Jerry is a very good father, doing his share in caring for the babies. He and Mrs. Jerry are rather social and enjoy visiting neighbors of their own kind. Their voices are a sort of squeak, and you can often hear them talking among the rushes in the early evening. That is the hour they like best, though they are abroad during the day when undisturbed. Man is their greatest enemy. He hunts and traps them for their warm coats. But they have to watch out for Hooty the Owl at night and for Reddy Fox and Old Man Coyote whenever they are on land. Billy Mink also is an enemy at times, perhaps the most to be dreaded because he can follow Jerry anywhere.

"Jerry makes little landings of mud and rushes along the edge of the shore. On these he delights to sit to eat his meals. He likes apples and vegetables and sometimes will travel quite a distance to get them. Late in the summer he begins to prepare for winter by starting work on his house, if he is to have a new one. He is a good worker. There isn't a lazy bone in him. All things considered, Jerry is a credit to his family.

"But if Jerry is a credit to his family there is one of its members who is not and that is—who knows?"

"Robber the Brown Rat," replied Happy Jack Squirrel promptly. "I have often seen him around Farmer Brown's barn. Ugh! He is an ugly-looking fellow."

"And he is just as ugly as he looks," replied Old Mother Nature. "There isn't a good thing I can say for him, not one. He doesn't belong in this country at all. He was brought here by man, and now he is found everywhere. He is sometimes called the Norway Rat and sometimes the Wharf Rat and House Rat. He is hated by all animals and by man. He is big, being next in size to Jerry Muskrat, savage in temper, the most destructive of any animal I know, and dirty in his habits. He is an outcast, but he doesn't seem to care.

"He lives chiefly around the homes of men, and all his food is stolen. That is why he is named Robber. He eats anything he can find and isn't the least bit particular what it is or whether it be clean or unclean. He gnaws into grain bins and steals the grain. He gets into hen-houses and sucks the eggs and kills young chickens. He would like nothing better than to find a nest of your babies, Peter Rabbit."

Peter shivered. "I'm glad he sticks to the homes of men," said he.

"But he doesn't," declared Old Mother Nature. "Often in summer he moves out into the fields, digging burrows there and doing great damage to crops and also killing and eating any of the furred and feathered folk he can catch. But he is not fond of the light of day. His deeds are deeds of darkness, and he prefers dark places. He has very large families, sometimes ten or more babies at a time, and several families in a year. That is why his tribe has managed to overrun the Great World and why they cause such great damage. Worse than the harm they do with their teeth is the terrible harm they do to man by carrying dreadful diseases and spreading them— diseases which cause people to die in great numbers."

"Isn't Robber afraid of any one?" asked Peter.

"He certainly is," replied Old Mother Nature. "He is in deadly fear of one whom every one of you fears—Shadow the Weasel. One good thing I can say for Shadow is that he never misses a chance to kill a Rat. Wherever a Rat can go he can go, and once he finds a colony he hunts them until he has killed all or driven them away.

"When food becomes scarce, Robber and his family move on to where it is more plentiful. Often they make long journeys, a great number of them together, and do not hesitate to swim a stream that may be in their path."

"I've never seen Robber," said Peter. "What kind of a tail does he have?"

"I might have known you would ask that," laughed Old Mother Nature. "It is long and slim and has no hair on it. His fur is very coarse and harsh and is brown and gray. He has a close relative called the Black Rat. But the latter is smaller and has been largely driven out of the country by his bigger cousin. Now I guess this is enough about Robber. He is bad, all bad, and hasn't a single friend in all the Great World."

"What a dreadful thing—not to have a single friend," said Happy Jack.

"It is dreadful, very dreadful," replied Old Mother Nature. "But it is wholly his own fault. It shows what happens when one becomes dishonest and bad at heart. The worst of it is Robber doesn't care. To-morrow I'll tell you about some of his cousins who are not bad."

CHAPTER XIV
A Trader and a Handsome Fellow

"Way down in the Sunny South," began Old Mother Nature, "lives a member of the Rat family who, though not nearly so bad as Robber, is none too good and so isn't thought well of at all. He is Little Robber the Cotton Rat, and though small for a Rat, being only a trifle larger than Striped Chipmunk, looks the little savage that he is. He has short legs and is rather thick-bodied, and appears much like an overgrown Meadow Mouse with a long tail. The latter is not bare like Robber's, but the hair on it is very short and thin. In color he is yellowish-brown and whitish underneath. His fur is longer and coarser than that of other native Rats.

"He lives in old fields, along ditches and hedges, and in similar places where there is plenty of cover in which he can hide from his enemies. He burrows in the ground and usually has his nest of dry grass there, though often in summer it is the surface of the ground. He does not live in and around the homes of men, like the Brown Rat, but he causes a great deal of damage by stealing grain in the shock. He eats all kinds of grain, many seeds, and meat when he can get it. He is very destructive to eggs and young of ground-nesting birds. He has a bad temper and will fight savagely. Mr. and Mrs. Cotton Rat raise several large families in a year. Foxes, Owls and Hawks are their chief enemies.

"But there are other members of the Rat family far more interesting and quite worth knowing. One of these is Trader the Wood Rat, in some parts of the Far West called the Pack Rat. Among the mountains he is called the Mountain Rat. Wherever found, his habits are much the same and make him one of the most interesting of all the little people who wear fur.

"Next to Jerry Muskrat he is the largest native Rat, that

is, of the Rats which belong in this country. He is about two thirds as big as Robber the Brown Rat, but though he is of the same general shape, so that you would know at once that he is related to Robber, he is in all other ways wholly unlike that outcast. His fur is thick and soft, almost as soft as that of a Squirrel. His fairly long tail is covered with hair. Indeed, some members of his branch of the family have tails almost as bushy as a Squirrel's. His coat is soft gray and a yellowish-brown above, and underneath pure white or light buff. His feet are white. He has rounded ears and big black eyes with none of the ugliness in them that you always see in the eyes of Robber. And he has long whiskers and plenty of them."

"But why is he called Trader?" asked Rabbit a bit impatiently.

"Patience, Peter, patience. I'm coming to that," chided Old Mother Nature. "He is Trader because his greatest delight is in trading. He is a born trader if ever there was one. He doesn't steal as other members of his family but trades. He puts something back in place of whatever he takes. It may be little sticks or chips or pebbles or anything else that is handy but it is something to replace what he has taken. You see, he is very honest. If Trader finds something belonging to some one else that he wants he takes it, but he tries to pay for it.

"Next to trading he delights in collecting. His home is a regular museum. He delights in anything bright and shiny. When he can get into the camps of men he will take anything he can move. But being honest, he tries to leave something in return. All sorts of queer things are found in his home—buckles cut from saddles, spoons, knives, forks, even money he has taken from the pockets of sleeping campers. Whenever any small object is missed from a camp, the first place visited in search of it is the home of Trader. In the mountains he sometimes makes piles of little pebbles just for the fun of collecting them.

"He is found all over the West, from the mountains to the deserts, in thick forests and on sandy wastes. He is also found in parts of the East and in the Sunny South. He is a great climber and is perfectly at home in trees or among rocks. He eats seeds, grain, many kinds of nuts, leaves and other parts of plants. In the colder sections he lays up stores for winter."

"What kind of a home does he have?" asked Happy Jack.

"His home usually is a very remarkable affair," replied Old Mother Nature. "It depends largely on where he is. When he is living in rocky country, he makes it amongst the rocks. In some places he burrows in the ground. But more often it is on the surface of the ground—a huge pile of sticks and thorns in the very middle of which is his snug, soft nest. The sticks and thorns are to protect it from enemies. When he lives down where cactus grow, those queer plants with long sharp spines, he uses these, and there are few enemies who will try to pull one of these houses apart to get at him.

"When he is alarmed or disturbed, he has a funny habit of drumming on the ground with his hind feet in much the same way that Peter Rabbit and Jumper the Hare thump, only he does it rapidly. Sometimes he builds his house in a tree. When he finds a cabin in the woods he at once takes possession, carrying in a great mass of sticks and trash. He is chiefly active at night, and a very busy fellow he is, trading and collecting. He has none of the mean disposition of Robber the Brown Rat. Mrs. Trader has two to five babies at a time and raises several families in a year. As I said before, Trader is one of the most interesting little people I know of, and he does very, very funny things.

"Now we come to the handsomest member of the family, Longfoot the Kangaroo Rat, so called because of his long hind legs and tail and the way in which he sits up and jumps. Really he is not a member of the Rat branch of the family, but closely related to the Pocket Mice. You see, he has pockets in his cheeks."

"Like mine?" asked Striped Chipmunk quickly.

"No, they are on the outside instead of the inside of his cheeks. Yours are inside."

"I think mine must be a lot handier," asserted Striped Chipmunk, nodding his head in a very decided way.

"Longfoot seems to think his are quite satisfactory," replied Old Mother Nature. "He really is handsome, but he isn't a bit vain and is very gentle. He never tries to bite when caught and taken in a man's hand."

"But you haven't told us how big he is or what he looks like," protested impatient Peter.

"When he sits up or jumps he looks like a tiny Kangaroo. But that doesn't mean anything to you, and you are no wiser than before, for you never have seen a Kangaroo," replied Old Mother Nature. "In the first place he is about the size of Striped Chipmunk. That is, his body is about the size of Striped Chipmunk's; but his tail is longer than his head and body together."

"My, it must be some tail!" exclaimed Peter Rabbit admiringly.

Old Mother Nature smiled. "It is," said she. "You would like that tail, Peter. His front legs are short and the feet small, but his hind legs are long and the feet big. Of course you have seen Nimbleheels the Jumping Mouse, Peter."

Peter nodded. "Of course," he replied. "My how that fellow can jump!"

"Well, Longfoot is built on the same plan as Nimbleheels and for the same purpose," continued Old Mother Nature. "He is a jumper."

"Then I know what that long tail is for," cried Peter. "It is to keep him balanced when he is in the air so that he can jump straight."

"Right again, Peter," laughed Old Mother Nature. "That is just what it is for. Without it, he never would know where he was going to land when he jumped. As I told you, he is a handsome little fellow. His fur is very soft and silky. Above, it is a pretty yellowish-brown, but underneath it is pure white. His cheeks are brown, he is white around the ears, and a white stripe crosses his hips and keeps right on along the sides of his tail. The upper and under parts of his tail are almost or quite black, and the tail ends in a tuft of long hair which is pure white. His feet are also white. His head is rather large for his size, and long. He has a long nose. Longfoot has a number of cousins, some of them much smaller than he, but they all look very much alike."

"Where do they live?" asked Johnny Chuck, for Johnny had been unable to stay away from school another day.

"In the dry, sandy parts of the Southwest, places so dry that it seldom rains, and water is to be found only long distances apart," replied Old Mother Nature.

"Then how does Longfoot get water to drink?" demanded Chatterer the Red Squirrel.

"He gets along without drinking," replied Old Mother Nature. "Such moisture as he needs he gets from his food. He eats seeds, leaves of certain plants and tender young plants just coming up. He burrows in the ground and throws up large mounds of earth. These have several entrances. One of these is the main entrance, and during the day this is often kept closed with earth. Under the mound he has little tunnels in all directions, a snug little bedroom and storerooms for food. He is very industrious and dearly loves to dig.

"Longfoot likes to visit his relatives sometimes, and where there are several families living near together, little paths lead from mound to mound. He comes out mostly at night, probably because he feels it to be safer then. Then, too, in that hot country it is cooler at night. The dusk of early evening is his favorite playtime. If Longfoot has a quarrel with one of his relatives they fight, hopping about each other, watching for a chance to leap and kick with those long, strong hind feet. Longfoot sometimes drums with his hind feet after the manner of Trader the Wood Rat.

"Now I think this will do for this morning. If any of you should meet Whitefoot the Wood Mouse, tell him to come to school to-morrow morning. And you might tell Danny Meadow if you little folks want school to continue."

"We do!" cried Peter Rabbit and Jumper the Hare and Happy Jack Squirrel and Chatterer the Red Squirrel and Striped Chipmunk and Johnny Chuck as one.

WHITEFOOT THE WOOD MOUSE. One of the prettiest members of the Mouse family.

TRADER THE WOOD RAT. This is the Eastern form of this interesting branch of the Rat family.

CHAPTER XV
TWO UNLIKE LITTLE COUSINS

Whitefoot the Wood Mouse is one of the smallest of the little people who live in the Green Forest. Being so small he is one of the most timid. You see, by day and by night sharp eyes are watching for Whitefoot and he knows it. Never one single instant, while he is outside where sharp eyes of hungry enemies may see him, does he forget that they are watching for him. To forget even for one little minute might mean—well, it might mean the end of little Whitefoot, but a dinner for some one with a liking for tender Mouse.

So Whitefoot the Wood Mouse rarely ventures more than a few feet from a hiding place and safety. At the tiniest sound he starts nervously and often darts back into hiding without waiting to find out if there really is any danger. If he waited to make sure he might wait too long, and it is better to be safe than sorry. If you and I had as many real frights in a year, not to mention false frights, as Whitefoot has in a day, we would, I suspect, lose our minds. Certainly we would be the most unhappy people in all the Great World.

But Whitefoot isn't unhappy. Not a bit of it. He is a very happy little fellow. There is a great deal of wisdom in that pretty little head of his. There is more real sense in it than in some very big heads. When some of his neighbors make fun of him for being so very, very timid he doesn't try to pretend that he isn't afraid. He doesn't get angry. He simply says:

"Of course I'm timid, very timid indeed. I'm afraid of almost everything. I would be foolish not to be. It is because I am afraid that I am alive and happy right now. I hope I shall never be less timid than I am now, for it would mean that sooner or later I would fail to run in time and would be gobbled up. It isn't cowardly to be timid when there is danger all around. Nor is it bravery to take a foolish and needless risk. So I seldom go far from home. It isn't safe for me, and I know it."

This being the way Whitefoot looked at matters, you can guess how he felt when Chatterer the Red Squirrel caught sight of him and gave him Old Mother Nature's message.

"Hi there, Mr. Fraidy!" shouted Chatterer, as he caught sight of Whitefoot darting under a log. "Hi there! I've got a message for you!"

Slowly, cautiously, Whitefoot poked his head out from beneath the old log and looked up at Chatterer. "What kind of a message?" he demanded suspiciously.

"A message you'll do well to heed. It is from Old Mother Nature," replied Chatterer.

"A message from Old Mother Nature!" cried Whitefoot, and came out a bit more from beneath the old log.

"That's what I said, a message from Old Mother Nature, and if you will take my advice you will heed it," retorted Chatterer. "She says you are to come to school with the rest of us at sun-up to-morrow morning."

Then Chatterer explained about the school and where it was held each morning and what a lot he and his friends had already learned there. Whitefoot listened with something very like dismay in his heart. That place where school was held was a long way off. That is, it was a long way for him, though to Peter Rabbit or Jumper the Hare it wouldn't have seemed long at all. It meant that he would have to leave all his hiding places and the thought made him shiver.

But Old Mother Nature had sent for him and not once did he even think of disobeying. "Did you say that school begins at sun-up?" he asked, and when Chatterer nodded Whitefoot sighed. It was a sigh of relief. "I'm glad of that," said he. "I can travel in the night, which will be much safer. I'll be there. That is, I will if I am not caught on the way."

Meanwhile over on the Green Meadows Peter Rabbit was looking for Danny Meadow Mouse. Danny's home was not far from the dear Old Briar-patch, and he and Peter were and still are very good friends. So Peter knew just about where to look for Danny and it didn't take him long to find him.

"Hello, Peter! You look as if you have something very important on your mind," was the greeting of Danny Meadow Mouse as Peter came hurrying up.

"I have," said Peter. "It is a message for you. Old Mother Nature says for you to be on hand at sun-up to-morrow when school opens over in the Green Forest. Of course you will be there."

"Of course," replied Danny in the most matter-of-fact tone. "Of course. If Old Mother Nature really sent me that message—"

"She really did," interrupted Peter.

"There isn't anything for me to do but obey," finished Danny. Then his face became very sober. "That is a long way for me to go, Peter," said he. "I wouldn't take such a long journey for anything or for anybody else. Old Mother Nature knows, and if she sent for me she must be sure I can make the trip safely. What time did you say I must be there?"

"At sun-up," replied Peter. "Shall I call for you on my way there?"

Danny shook his head. Then he began to laugh. "What are you laughing at?" demanded Peter.

"At the very idea of me with my short legs trying to keep up with you," replied Danny. "I wish you would sit up and take a good look all around to make sure that Old Man Coyote and Reddy Fox and Redtail the Hawk and Black Pussy, that pesky Cat from Farmer Brown's, are nowhere about."

Peter obligingly sat up and looked this way and looked that way and looked the other way. No one of whom he or Danny Meadow Mouse need be afraid was to be seen. He said as much, then asked, "Why did you want to know, Danny?"

"Because I am going to start at once," replied Danny.

"Start for where?" asked Peter, looking much puzzled.

"Start for school of course," replied Danny rather shortly.

"But school doesn't begin until sun-up to-morrow," protested Peter.

"Which is just the reason I am going to start now," retorted Danny. "If I should put off starting until the last minute I might not get there at all. I would have to hurry, and it is difficult to hurry and watch for danger at the same time. I've noticed that people who put things off to the last minute and then have to hurry are quite apt to rush headlong into trouble. The way is clear now, so I am going to start. I can take my time and keep a proper watch for danger. I'll see you over there in the morning, Peter."

Danny turned and disappeared in one of his private little paths though the tall grass. Peter noticed that he was headed towards the Green Forest.

When Peter and the others arrived for school the next morning they found Whitefoot the Wood Mouse and Danny Meadow Mouse waiting with Old Mother Nature. Safe in her presence, they seemed to have lost much of their usual timidity. Whitefoot was sitting on the end of a log and Danny was on the ground just beneath him.

"I want all the rest of you to look well at these two little cousins and notice how unlike two cousins can be," said Old Mother Nature. "Whitefoot, who is quite as often called Deer Mouse as Wood Mouse, is one of the prettiest of the entire Mouse family. I suspect he is called Deer Mouse because the upper part of his coat is such a beautiful fawn color. Notice that the upper side of his long slim tail is of the same color, while the under side is white, as is the whole under part of Whitefoot. Also those dainty feet are white, hence his name. See what big, soft black eyes he has, and notice that those delicate ears are of good size.

"His tail is covered with short fine hairs, instead of being naked as is the tail of Nibbler the House mouse, of whom I will tell you later. Whitefoot loves the Green

Forest, but out in parts of the Far West where there is no Green Forest he lives on the brushy plains. He is a good climber and quite at home in the trees. There he seems almost like a tiny Squirrel. Tell us, Whitefoot, where you make your home and what you eat."

"My home just now," replied Whitefoot, "is in a certain hollow in a certain dead limb of a certain tree. I suspect that a member of the Woodpecker family made that hollow, but no one was living there when I found it. Mrs. Whitefoot and I have made a soft, warm nest there and wouldn't trade homes with any one. We have had our home in a hollow log on the ground, in an old stump, in a hole we dug in the ground under a rock, and in an old nest of some bird. That was in a tall bush. We roofed that nest over and made a little round doorway on the under side. Once we raised a family in a box in a dark corner of Farmer Brown's sugar camp.

"I eat all sorts of things—seeds, nuts, insects and meat when I can get it. I store up food for winter, as all wise and thrifty people do."

"I suppose that means that you do not sleep as Johnny Chuck does in winter," remarked Peter Rabbit.

"I should say not!" exclaimed Whitefoot. "I like winter. It is fun to run about on the snow. Haven't you ever seen my tracks, Peter?"

"I have, lots of times," spoke up Jumper the Hare. "Also I've seen you skipping about after dark. I guess you don't care much for sunlight."

"I don't," replied Whitefoot. "I sleep most of the time during the day, and work and play at night. I feel safer then. But on dull days I often come out. It is the bright sunlight I don't like. That is one reason I stick to the Green Forest. I don't see how Cousin Danny stands it out there on the Green Meadows. Now I guess it is his turn."

Every one looked at Danny Meadow Mouse. In appearance he was as unlike Whitefoot as it was possible to be and still be a Mouse. There was nothing pretty or graceful about Danny. He wasn't dainty at all. His body was rather stout, looking stouter than it really was because his fur was quite long. His head was blunt, and he seemed to have no neck at all, though of course he did have one. His eyes were small, like little black beads. His ears were almost hidden in his hair. His legs were short and his tail was quite short, as if it had been cut off when half grown. No, those two cousins didn't look a bit alike. Danny felt most uncomfortable as the others compared him with pretty Whitefoot. He knew he was homely, but never before had he felt it quite so keenly. Old Mother Nature saw and understood.

"It isn't how we look, but what we are and what we do and how we fit into our particular places in life that count," said she. "Now, Danny is a homely little fellow, but I know, and I know that he knows that he is just fitted for the life he lives, and he lives it more successfully for being just as he is.

"Danny is a lover of the fields and meadows where there is little else but grass in which to hide. Everything about him is just suited for living there. Isn't that so, Danny?"

"Yes'm, I guess so," replied Danny. "Sometimes my tail does seem dreadfully short to look well."

Everybody laughed, even Danny himself. Then he remembered how once Reddy Fox had so nearly caught him that one of Reddy's black paws had touched the tip of his tail. Had that tail been any longer Reddy would have caught him by it. Danny's face cleared and he hastened to declare, "After all, my tail suits me just as it is."

"Wisely spoken, Danny," said Old Mother Nature. "Now it is your turn to tell how you live and what you eat and anything else of interest about yourself."

"I guess there isn't much interesting about me," began Danny modestly. "I'm just one of the plain, common little folks. I guess everybody knows me so well there is nothing for me to tell."

"Some of them may know all about you, but I don't," declared Jumper the Hare. "I never go out on the Green

Meadows where you live. How do you get about in all that tall grass?"

"Oh, that's easy enough," replied Danny. "I cut little paths in all directions."

"Just the way I do in the dear Old Briar-patch," interrupted Peter Rabbit.

"I keep those little paths clear and clean so that there never is anything in my way to trip me up when I have to run for safety," continued Danny. "When the grass gets tall those little paths are almost like little tunnels. The time I dread most is when Farmer Brown cuts the grass for hay. I not only have to watch out for that dreadful mowing machine, but when the hay has been taken away the grass is so short that it is hard work for me to keep out of sight.

"I sometimes dig a short burrow and at the end of it make a nice nest of dry grass. Sometimes in summer Mrs. Danny and I make our nest on the surface of the ground in a hollow or in a clump of tall grass, especially if the ground is low and wet. We have several good-sized families in a year. All Meadow Mice believe in large families, and that is probably why there are more Meadow Mice than any other Mice in the country. I forgot to say that I am also called Field Mouse."

"And it is because there are so many of your family and they require so much to eat that you do a great deal of damage to grass and other crops," spoke up Old Mother Nature. "You see," she explained to the others, "Danny eats grass, clover, bulbs, roots, seeds and garden vegetables. He also eats some insects. He sometimes puts away a few seeds for the winter, but depends chiefly on finding enough to eat, for he is active all winter. He tunnels about under the snow in search of food. When other food is hard to find he eats bark, and then he sometimes does great damage in young orchards. He gnaws the bark from young fruit trees all the way around as high as he can reach, and of course this kills the trees. He is worse than Peter Rabbit.

"Danny didn't mention that he is a good swimmer and

not at all afraid of the water. No one has more enemies than he, and the fact that he is alive and here at school this morning is due to his everlasting watchfulness. This will do for to-day. To-morrow we will take up others of the Mouse family."

CHAPTER XVI
Danny's Northern Cousins and Nimbleheels

Whitefoot the Wood Mouse and Danny Meadow Mouse had become so interested that they decided they couldn't afford to miss the next lesson. Neither did either of them feel like making the long journey to his home and back again. So Whitefoot found a hole in a stump near by and decided to camp out there for a few days. Danny decided to do the same thing in a comfortable place under a pile of brush not far away. So the next morning both were on hand when school opened.

"I told you yesterday that I would tell you about some of Danny's cousins," began Old Mother Nature just as Chatterer the Red Squirrel, who was late, came hurrying up quite out of breath. "Way up in the Far North are two of Danny's cousins more closely related to him than to any other members of the Mouse family. Yet, strange to say, they are not called Mice at all, but Lemmings. However, they belong to the Mouse family.

"Bandy the Banded Lemming is the most interesting, because he is the one member of the entire family who changes the color of his coat. In summer he wears beautiful shades of reddish brown and gray, but in winter his coat is wholly white. He is also called the Hudson Bay Lemming.

"Danny Meadow Mouse thinks his tail is short, but he wouldn't if he should see Bandy's tail. That is so short it hardly shows beyond his long fur. He is about Danny's size, but a little stouter and stockier, and his long fur makes him appear even thicker-bodied than he really is. He has very short legs, and his ears are so small that they are quite hidden in the fur around them, so that he appears to have no ears at all.

"In that same far northern country is a close relative called the Brown Lemming. He is very much like Bandy save that he is all brown and does not change his coat in

THE BROWN LEMMING. A norther cousin of Danny Meadow Mouse.

winter. Both have the same general habits, and these are much like the habits of Danny Meadow Mouse. They make short burrows in the ground leading to snug, warm nests of grass and moss. In winter they make little tunnels in every direction under the snow, with now and then an opening to the surface.

"There are many more Brown Lemmings than Banded Lemmings, and their little paths run everywhere through the grass and moss. In that country there is a great deal of moss. It covers the ground just as grass does here. But the most interesting thing about these Lemmings is the way they migrate. To migrate is to move from one part of the country to another. You know most of the birds migrate to the Sunny South every autumn and back every spring.

"Once in a while it happens that food becomes very scarce where the Lemmings are. Then very many of them get together, just as migrating birds form great flocks, and start on a long journey in search of a place where there is plenty of food. They form a great army and push ahead, regardless of everything. They swim wide rivers and even lakes which may lie in their way. Of course, they eat everything eatable in their path."

"My!" exclaimed Danny Meadow Mouse, "I'm glad I don't live in a country where I might have to make such long journeys. I don't envy those cousins up there in the Far North a bit. I'm perfectly satisfied to live right on the Green Meadows."

"Which shows your good common sense," said Old Mother Nature. "By the way, Danny, I suppose you are acquainted with Nimbleheels the Jumping Mouse, who also is rather fond of the Green Meadows. I ought to have sent word to him to be here this morning."

Hardly were the words out of Old Mother Nature's mouth when something landed in the leaves almost at her feet and right in the middle of school. Instantly Danny Meadow Mouse scurried under a pile of dead leaves. Whitefoot the Wood Mouse darted into a knothole in the log on which he had been sitting. Jumper the Hare dodged behind a little hemlock tree. Peter Rabbit bolted for a hollow log. Striped Chipmunk vanished in a hole under an old stump. Johnny Chuck backed up against the trunk of a tree and made ready to fight. Only Happy Jack the Gray Squirrel and Chatterer the Red Squirrel and Prickly Porky the Porcupine, who were sitting in trees, kept their places. You see they felt quite safe.

As soon as all those who had run had reached places of safety, they peeped out to see what had frightened them so. Just imagine how very, very foolish they felt when they saw Old Mother Nature smiling down at a little fellow just about the size of little Whitefoot, but with a much longer tail. It was Nimbleheels the Jumping Mouse.

"Well, well, well," exclaimed Old Mother Nature. "I was just speaking of you and wishing I had you here. How did you happen to come? And what do you mean by scaring my pupils half out of their wits?" Her eyes twinkled. Nimbleheels saw this and knew that she was only pretending to be severe.

Before he could reply Johnny Chuck began to chuckle. The chuckle became a laugh, and presently Johnny was laughing so hard he had to hold his sides. Now, as you know, laughter is catching. In a minute or so everybody was laughing, and no one but Johnny Chuck knew what the joke was. At last Peter Rabbit stopped laughing long enough to ask Johnny what he was laughing at.

"At the idea of that little pinch of nothing giving us all such a fright," replied Johnny Chuck. Then all laughed some more.

When they were through laughing Nimbleheels answered Old Mother Nature's questions. He explained that he had heard about that school, as by this time almost every one in the Green Forest and on the Green Meadows had. By chance he learned that Danny Meadow Mouse was attending. He thought that if it was a good thing for Danny it would be a good thing for him, so he had come.

"Just as I was almost here I heard a twig snap behind me, or thought I did, and I jumped so as to get here and be safe. I didn't suppose anyone would be frightened by little me," he explained. "It was some jump!" exclaimed Jumper the Hare admiringly. "He went right over my head, and I was sitting up at that!"

"It isn't much of a jump to go over your head," replied Nimbleheels. "You ought to see me when I really try to jump. I wasn't half trying when I landed here. I'm sorry I frightened all of you so. It gives me a queer feeling just to think that I should be able to frighten anybody. If you please, Mother Nature, am I in time for to-day's lesson?"

"Not for all of it, but you are just in time for the part I wanted you here for," replied Old Mother Nature. "Hop up on that log side of your Cousin Whitefoot, where all can see you."

Nimbleheels hopped up beside Whitefoot the Wood Mouse, and as the two little cousins sat side by side they were not unlike in general appearance, though of the two Whitefoot was the prettier. The coat of Nimbleheels was a dull yellowish, darker on the back than on the sides. Like Whitefoot he was white underneath. His ears were much smaller than those of Whitefoot. But the greatest differences between the two were in their hind legs and tails.

The hind legs and feet of Nimbleheels were long, on the same plan as those of Peter Rabbit. From just a glance at them any one would know that he was a born jumper and a good one. Whitefoot possessed a long tail, but the tail of Nimbleheels was much longer, slim and tapering.

"There," said Old Mother Nature, "is the greatest jumper for his size among all the animals in this great country. When I say this, I mean the greatest ground jumper. Timmy the Flying Squirrel jumps farther, but Timmy has to climb to a high place and then coasts down on the air. I told you what wonderful jumps Jack Rabbit can make, but if he could jump as high and far for his size as Nimbleheels can jump for his size, the longest jump Jack has ever made would seem nothing more than a hop. By the way, both Nimbleheels and Whitefoot have small pockets in their cheeks. Tell us where you live, Nimbleheels."

"I live among the weeds along the edge of the Green Meadows," replied Nimbleheels, "though sometimes I go way out on the Green Meadows. But I like best to be among the weeds because they are tall and keep me well hidden, and also because they furnish me plenty to eat. You see, I live largely on seeds, though I am also fond of berries and small nuts, especially beechnuts. Some of my family prefer the Green Forest, especially if there is a Laughing Brook or pond in it. Personally I prefer, as I said before, the edge of the Green Meadows."

"Do you make your home under the ground?" asked Striped Chipmunk.

"For winter, yes," replied Nimbleheels. "In summer I sometimes put my nest just a few inches under ground, but often I hide it under a piece of bark or in a thick clump of grass, just as Danny Meadow Mouse often does his. In the fall I dig a deep burrow, deep enough to be beyond the reach of Jack Frost, and in a nice little bedroom down there I sleep the winter away. I have little storerooms down there too, in which I put seeds, berries and nuts. Then when I do wake up I have plenty to eat."

"I might add," said Old Mother Nature, "that when he goes to sleep for the winter he curls up in a little ball with his long tail wrapped around him, and in his bed of soft grass he sleeps very sound indeed. Like Johnny Chuck he gets very fat before going to sleep. Now, Nimbleheels, show us how you can jump."

Nimbleheels hopped down from the log on which he had been sitting and at once shot into the air in such a high, long, beautiful jump that everybody exclaimed. This way and that way he went in great leaps. It was truly wonderful.

"That long tail is what balances him," explained Old Mother Nature. "If he should lose it he would simply turn over and over and never know where or how he was going to land. His jumping is done only in times of danger. When he is not alarmed he runs about on the ground like the rest of the Mouse family. This is all for to-day. To-morrow I will tell you still more about the Mouse family."

NIMBLEHEELS THE JUMPING MOUSE. Look for this pretty little fellow in old weedy fields.

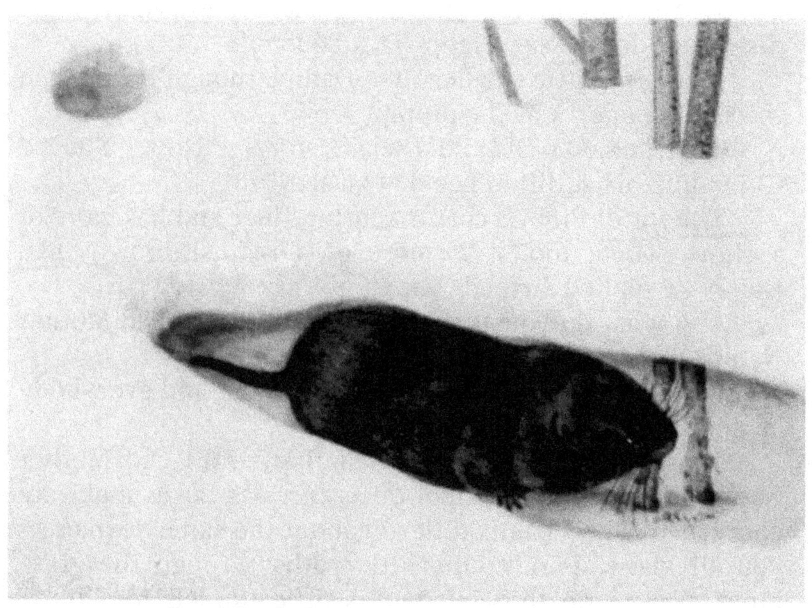

DANNY MEADOW MOUSE. He kills young trees by gnawing off the bark under the snow.

CHAPTER XVII
THREE LITTLE REDCOATS AND SOME OTHERS

With Whitefoot the Wood Mouse, Danny Meadow Mouse and Nimbleheels the Jumping Mouse attending school, the Mouse family was well represented, but when school opened the morning after Nimbleheels had made his sudden and startling appearance, there was still another present. It was Piney the Pine Mouse. Whitefoot, who knew him, had hunted him up and brought him along.

"I thought you wouldn't mind if Piney came," explained Whitefoot.

"I'm glad he has come," replied Old Mother Nature. "It is much better to see a thing than merely to be told about it, and now you have a chance to see for yourselves the differences between two cousins very closely related, Danny Meadow Mouse and Piney the Pine Mouse. What difference do you see, Happy Jack Squirrel?"

"Piney is a little smaller than Danny, though he is much the same shape," was the prompt reply.

"True," said Old Mother Nature. "Now, Striped Chipmunk, what difference do you see?"

"The fur of Piney's coat is shorter, finer and has more of a shine. Then, too, it is more of a reddish-brown than Danny's," replied Striped Chipmunk.

"And what do you say, Peter Rabbit?" asked Old Mother Nature.

"Piney has a shorter tail," declared Peter, and everybody laughed.

"Trust you to look at his tail first," said Old Mother Nature. "These are the chief differences as far as looks are concerned. Their habits differ in about the same degree. As you all know, Danny cuts little paths through the grass. Piney doesn't do this, but makes little tunnels just under the surface of the ground very much as Miner the Mole does. He isn't fond of the open Green Meadows or of damp places as Danny is, but likes best the edge of the Green Forest and brushy places. He is very much at home in a poorly kept orchard where the weeds are allowed to grow and in young orchards he does a great deal of damage by cutting off the roots of young trees and stripping off the bark as high up as he can reach. Tell us, Piney, how and where you make your home."

Piney hesitated a little, for he was bashful. "I make my home under ground," he ventured finally. "I dig a nice little bedroom with several entrances from my tunnels, and in it I make a fine nest of soft grass. Close by I dig one or more rooms in which to store my food, and these usually are bigger than my bedroom. When I get one filled with food I close it up by filling the entrance with earth."

"What do you put in your storerooms?" asked Peter Rabbit.

"Short pieces of grass and pieces of roots of different kinds," replied Piney. "I am very fond of tender roots and the bark of trees and bushes.

"And he dearly loves to get in a garden where he can tunnel along a row of potatoes or other root crops," added Old Mother Nature. "Because of these habits he does a great deal of damage and is much disliked by man. Striped Chipmunk mentioned his reddish-brown coat. There is another cousin with a coat so red that he is called the Red-backed Mouse. He is about the size of Danny Meadow Mouse but has larger ears and a longer tail.

"This little fellow is a lover of the Green Forest, and he is quite as active by day as by night. He is pretty, especially when he sits up to eat, holding his food in his paws as does Happy Jack Squirrel. He makes his home in a burrow, the entrance to which is under an old stump, a rock or the root of a tree. His nest is of soft grass or moss. Sometimes he makes it in a hollow log or stump instead of digging a bedroom under ground. He is thrifty and lays up a supply of food in underground rooms, hollow logs and similar places. He eats seeds, small fruits, roots and various plants. Because of his preference for the Green Forest and the fact that he lives as a rule far from the homes of men, he does little real damage.

"There is still another little Redcoat in the family, and he is especially interesting because while he is related to Danny Meadow Mouse he lives almost wholly in trees. He is called the Rufous Tree Mouse. Rufous means reddish-brown, and he gets that name because of the color of his coat. He lives in the great forests of the Far West, where the trees are so big and tall that the biggest tree you have ever seen would look small beside them. And it is in those great trees that the Rufous Tree Mouse lives.

"Just why he took to living in trees no one knows, for he belongs to that branch of the family known as Ground Mice. But live in them he does, and he is quite as much at home in them as any Squirrel."

Chatterer the Red Squirrel was interested right away. "Does he build a nest in a tree like a Squirrel?" he asked.

"He certainly does," replied Old Mother Nature, "and often it is a most remarkable nest. In some sections he places it only in big trees, sometimes a hundred feet from the ground. In other sections it is placed in small trees and only a few feet above the ground. The high nests often are old deserted nests of Squirrels enlarged and built over. Some of them are very large indeed and have been used year after year. Each year they have been added to.

"One of these big nests will have several bedrooms and little passages running all through it. It appears that Mrs. Rufous usually has one of these big nests to herself, Rufous having a small nest of his own out on one of the branches. The big nest is close up against the trunk of the tree where several branches meet."

"Does Rufous travel from one tree to another, or does he live in just one tree?" asked Happy Jack Squirrel.

"Wherever branches of one tree touch those of another, and you know in a thick forest this is frequently the case, he travels about freely if he wants to. But those trees are so big that I suspect he spends most of his time in the one in which his home is," replied Old Mother Nature. "However, if an enemy appears in his home tree, he makes his escape by jumping from one tree to another, just as you would do."

"What I want to know is where he gets his food if he spends all his time up in the trees," spoke up Danny Meadow Mouse.

Old Mother Nature smiled. "Where should he get it but up where he lives?" she asked. "Rufous never has to worry about food. It is all around him. You see, so far as known, he lives wholly on the thick parts of the needles, which you know are the leaves, of fir and spruce trees, and on the bark of tender twigs. So you see he is more of a tree dweller than any of the Squirrel family. While Rufous has the general shape of Danny and his relatives, he has quite a long tail. Now I guess this will do for the nearest relatives of Danny Meadow Mouse."

"He certainly has a lot of them," remarked Whitefoot the Wood Mouse. Then he added a little wistfully, "Of course, in a way they are all cousins of mine, but I wish I had some a little more closely related."

"You have," replied Old Mother Nature, and Whitefoot pricked up his big ears. "One of them Bigear the Rock Mouse, who lives out in the mountains of the Far West. He is as fond of the rocks as Rufous is of the trees. Sometimes he lives in brush heaps and in brushy country, but he prefers rocks, and that is why he is known as the Rock Mouse.

"He is a pretty little fellow, if anything a trifle bigger than you, Whitefoot, and he is dressed much like you with a yellowish-brown coat and white waistcoat. He has just such a long tail covered with hair its whole length. But you should see his ears. He has the largest ears of any member of the whole family. That is why he is called Bigear. He likes best to be out at night, but often comes out on dull days. He eats seeds and small nuts and is especially fond of juniper seeds. He always lays up a supply of food for winter. Often he is found very high up on the mountains.

"Another of your cousins, Whitefoot, lives along the seashore of the East down in the Sunny South. He is called the Beach Mouse. In general appearance he is much like you, having the same shape, long tail and big ears, but he is a little smaller and his coat varies. When he lives back from the shore, in fields where the soil is dark, his upper coat is dark grayish-brown, but when he lives on the white sands of the seashore it is very light. His home is in short burrows in the ground.

"Now don't you little people think you have learned enough about the Mouse family?"

"You haven't told us about Nibbler the House Mouse yet. And you said you would," protested Peter Rabbit.

"And when we were learning about Longfoot the Kangaroo Rat you said he was most closely related to the Pocket Mice. What about them?" said Johnny Chuck.

Old Mother Nature laughed. "I see," said she, "that you want to know all there is to know. Be on hand to-morrow morning. I guess we can finish up with the Mouse family then and with them the order of Rodents to which all of you belong."

CHAPTER XVIII
MICE WITH POCKETS, AND OTHERS

"Pockets are very handy things for little people who are thrifty and who live largely on small seeds. Without pockets in which to carry the seeds, I am afraid some of them would never be able to store up enough food for winter," began Old Mother Nature, as soon as everybody was on hand the next morning.

"I wouldn't be without my pockets for any thing," spoke up Striped Chipmunk.

Old Mother Nature smiled. "You certainly do make good use of yours," said she. "But there are others who have even greater need of pockets, and among them are the Pocket Mice. Of course, it is because of their pockets that they are called Pocket Mice. All of these pretty little fellows live in the dry parts of the Far West and Southwest in the same region where Longfoot the Kangaroo Rat lives. They are close neighbors and relatives of his.

"Midget the Silky Pocket Mouse is one of the smallest animals in all the Great World, so small that Whitefoot the Wood Mouse is a giant compared with him. He weighs less than an ounce and is a dear little fellow. His back and sides are yellow, and beneath he is white. He has quite long hind legs and a long tail, and these show at once that he is a jumper. In each cheek is a pocket opening from the outside, and these pockets are lined with hair. He is called Silky Pocket Mouse because of the fineness and softness of his coat. He has some larger cousins, one of them being a little bigger than Nibbler the House Mouse. Neighbors and close relatives are the Spiny Pocket Mice."

"Do they have spines like Prickly Porky?" demanded Peter Rabbit.

Old Mother Nature laughed. "I don't wonder you ask," said she. "I think it is a foolish name myself, for they haven't any spines at all. Their fur isn't as fine as that of

NIBBLER THE HOUSE MOUSE. ROBBER THE BROWN RAT. Here are two of the worst pests in the world. Neither is native to America.

Midget, and it has all through it long coarse hairs almost like bristles, and from these they get their name. The smallest of the Spiny Pocket Mice is about the size of Nibbler the House Mouse and the largest is twice as big. They are more slender than their Silky cousins, and their tails are longer in proportion to their size and have little tufts of hair at the ends. Of course, they have pockets in their cheeks.

"In habits all the Pocket Mice are much alike. They make burrows in the ground, often throwing up a little mound with several entrances which lead to a central passageway connecting with the bedroom and storerooms. By day the entrances are closed with earth from inside, for the Mice are active only at night. Sometimes the burrows are hidden under bushes, and sometimes they are right out in the open. Living as they do in a hot, dry country, the Pocket Mice have learned to get along without drinking water. Their food consists mainly of a variety of small seeds.

"Another Mouse of the West looks almost enough like Whitefoot to be a member of his branch of the family. He has a beautiful yellowish-brown coat and white waistcoat, and his feet are white. But his tail is short in comparison with Whitefoot's and instead of being slim is quite thick. His fur is like velvet. He is called the Grasshopper Mouse."

"Is that because he eats Grasshoppers?" asked Peter Rabbit at once.

"You've guessed it," laughed Old Mother Nature. "He is very, very fond of Grasshoppers and Crickets. He eats many kinds of insects, Moths, Flies, Cutworms, Beetles, Lizards, Frogs and Scorpions. Because of his fondness for the latter he is called the Scorpion Mouse in some sections. He is fond of meat when he can get it. He also eats seeds of many kinds. He is found all over the West from well up in the North to the hot dry regions of the Southwest. When he cannot find a convenient deserted burrow of some other animal, he digs a home for himself and there raises several families each year. In the early evening he often utters a fine, shrill, whistling call note.

"Another little member of the Mouse family found clear across the country is the Harvest Mouse. He is never bigger than Nibbler the House Mouse and often is much smaller. In fact, he is one of the smallest of the entire family. In appearance he is much like Nibbler, but his coat is browner and there are fine hairs on his tail. He loves grassy, weedy or brushy places.

"As a rule he does little harm to man, for his food is chiefly seeds of weeds, small wild fruits and parts of wild plants of no value to man. Once in a while his family becomes so large that they do some damage in grain fields. But this does not happen often. The most interesting thing about this little Mouse is the way he builds his home. Sometimes he uses a hole in a tree or post and sometimes a deserted birds' nest, but more frequently he builds a nest for himself—a little round ball of grass and other vegetable matter. This is placed in thick grass or weeds close to the ground or in bushes or low trees several feet from the ground.

"They are well-built little houses and have one or more little doorways on the under side when they are in bushes or trees. Inside is a warm, soft bed made of milkweed or cattail down, the very nicest kind of a bed for the babies. No one has a neater home than the Harvest Mouse. He is quite as much at home in bushes and low trees as Happy Jack Squirrel is in bigger trees. His long tail comes in very handy then, for he often wraps it around a twig to make his footing more secure.

"Now this is all about the native Mice and—what is it, Peter?"

"You've forgotten Nibbler the House Mouse," replied Peter.

"How impatient some little folks are and how fearful that their curiosity will not be satisfied," remarked Old Mother Nature. "As I was saying, this is all about our native Mice; that is, the Mice who belong to this country. And now we come to Nibbler the House Mouse, who, like Robber the Brown Rat, has no business here at all, but who has followed man all over the world and like Robber has become a pest to man."

Peter Rabbit looked rather sheepish when he discovered that Old Mother Nature hadn't for gotten, and resolved that in the future he would hold his tongue.

"Have any of you seen Nibbler?" asked Old Mother Nature.

"I have," replied Danny Meadow Mouse. "Once I was carried to Farmer Brown's barn in a shock of corn and I found Nibbler living in the barn."

"It is a wonder he wasn't living in Farmer Brown's house," said Old Mother Nature. "Probably other members of his family were. He is perfectly at home in any building put up by man, just as is Robber the Rat. Because of his small size he can go where Robber cannot. He delights to scamper about between the walls. Being a true Rodent he is forever gnawing holes in the corners of rooms and opening on to pantry shelves so that he may steal food. He eats all sorts of food, but spoils more for man, by running about over it, than he eats. In barns and henhouses he gets into the grain bins and steals a great deal of grain.

"It is largely because of Robber the Rat and Nibbler that men keep the Cats you all hate so. A Cat is Nibbler's worst enemy. Nibbler is slender and graceful, with a long, hairless tail and ears of good size. He is very timid, ready to dart into his hole at the least sound. He raises from four to nine babies at a time and several sets of them in a year.

"If Mr. and Mrs. Nibbler are living in a house, their nest is made of scraps of paper, cloth, wool and other soft things stolen from the people who live in the house. In getting this material they often do great damage. If they are living in a barn, they make their nest of hay and any soft material they can find.

"While Nibbler prefers to live in or close to the homes of men, he sometimes is driven out and then takes to the fields, especially in summer. There he lives in all sorts of hiding places, and isn't at all particular what the place is, if it promises safety and food can be obtained close by. I'm sorry Nibbler ever came to this country. Man brought him here and now he is here to stay and quite as much at home as if he belonged here the way the rest of you do.

"This finishes the lessons on the order of Rodents, the animals related by reason of having teeth for the purpose of gnawing. I suspect these are the only ones in whom you take any interest, and so you will not care to come to school any more. Am I right?"

"No, marm," answered Happy Jack the Gray Squirrel, who, you remember, had laughed at Peter Rabbit for wanting to go to school. "No, marm. There are ever so many other people of the Green Forest and the Green Meadows we want to know more about than we now know. Isn't that so?" Happy Jack turned to the others and every one nodded, even Prickly Porky.

"There is one little fellow living right near here who looks to me as if he must be a member of the Mouse family, but he isn't like any of the Mice you have told us about," continued Happy Jack. "He is so small he can hide under a leaf. I'm sure he must be a Mouse."

"You mean Teeny Weeny the Shrew," replied Old Mother Nature, smiling at Happy Jack. "He isn't a Mouse. He isn't even a Rodent. I'll try to have him here to-morrow morning and we will see what we can find out about him and his relatives."

LONGFOOT THE KANGAROO RAT. He is not a true Rat but is related to the Pocket Mice.

DIGGER THE BADGER. Though he doesn't look it he is a member of the Weasel family.

TEENY WEENY THE SHREW. This is the common or long-tailed Shrew, one of the smallest animals in all the Great World.

THE SHORT-TAILED SHREW. He is sometimes called the Mole Shrew and the Blarina.

CHAPTER XIX
Teeny Weeny and His Cousin

"Of course Old Mother Nature knows, but just the same it is hard for me not to believe that Teeny Weeny is a member of the Mouse family," said Happy Jack Squirrel to Peter Rabbit, as they scampered along to school. "I never have had a real good look at him, but I've had glimpses of him lots of times and always supposed him a little Mouse with a short tail. It is hard to believe that he isn't."

"I hope Old Mother Nature will put him where we can get a good look at him," replied Peter. "Perhaps when you really see him he won't look so much like a Mouse."

When all had arrived Old Mother Nature began the morning lesson at once. "You have learned about all the families in the order of Rodents," said she, "so now we will take up another and much smaller order called Insectivora. I wonder if any of you can guess what that means."

"It sounds," said Peter Rabbit, "as if it must have something to do with insects."

"That is a very good guess, Peter," replied Old Mother Nature, smiling at him. "It does have to do with insects. The members of this order live very largely on insects and worms, and the name Insectivora means insect-eating. There are two families in this order, the Shrew family and the Mole family."

"Then Teeny Weeny and Miner the Mole must be related," spoke Peter quickly.

"Right again, Peter," was the prompt reply. "The Shrews and the Moles are related in the same way that you and Happy Jack Squirrel are related."

"And isn't Teeny Weeny the Shrew related to the Mice at all?" asked Happy Jack.

"Not at all," said Old Mother Nature. "Many people think he is and often he is called Shrew Mouse. But this is a great mistake. It is the result of ignorance. It seems strange to me that people so often know so little about their near neighbors." She looked at Happy Jack Squirrel as she said this, and Happy Jack looked sheepish. He felt just as he looked. All this time the eyes of every one had been searching this way, that way, every way, for Teeny Weeny, for Old Mother Nature had promised to try to have him there that morning. But Teeny Weeny was not to be seen. Now and then a leaf on the ground close by Old Mother Nature's feet moved, but the Merry Little Breezes were always stirring up fallen leaves, and no one paid any attention to these.

Old Mother Nature understood the disappointment in the faces before her and her eyes began to twinkle. "Yesterday I told you that I would try to have Teeny Weeny here," said she. A leaf moved. Stooping quickly she picked it up. "And here he is," she finished.

Sure enough where a second before the dead brown leaf had been was a tiny little fellow, so tiny that that leaf had covered him completely, and it wasn't a very big leaf. It was Teeny Weeny the Shrew, also called the Common Shrew, the Long-tailed Shrew and the Shrew Mouse, one of the smallest animals in all the Great World. He started to dart under another leaf, but Old Mother Nature stopped him. "Sit still," she commanded sharply. "You have nothing to fear. I want everybody to have a good look at you, for it is high time these neighbors of yours should know you. I know just how nervous and uncomfortable you are and I'll keep you only a few minutes. Now everybody take a good look at Teeny Weeny."

This command was quite needless, for all were staring with all their might. What they saw was a mite of a fellow less than four inches long from the tip of his nose to the tip of his tail, and of this total length the tail was almost half. He was slender, had short legs and mouselike feet. His coat was brownish above and grayish beneath, and the fur was very fine and soft.

But the oddest thing about Teeny Weeny was his long, pointed head ending in a long nose. No Mouse has a head like it. The edges of the ears could be seen above the fur, but the eyes were so tiny that Peter Rabbit thought he hadn't any and said so.

Old Mother Nature laughed. "Yes, he has eyes, Peter," said she. "Look closely and you will see them. But they don't amount to much—little more than to tell daylight from darkness. Teeny Weeny depends on his nose chiefly. He has a very wonderful little nose, flexible and very sensitive. Of course, with such poor eyes he prefers the dark when there are fewer enemies abroad."

All this time Teeny Weeny had been growing more and more uneasy. Old Mother Nature saw and understood. Now she told him that he might go. Hardly were the words out of her mouth when he vanished, darting under some dead leaves. Hidden by them he made his way to an old log and was seen no more.

"Doesn't he eat anything but insects and worms?" asked Striped Chipmunk.

"Yes," replied Old Mother Nature. "He is very fond of flesh, and if he finds the body of a bird or animal that has been killed he will tear it to pieces. He is very hot-tempered, as are all his family, and will not hesitate to attack a Mouse much bigger than himself. He is so little and so active that he has to have a great deal of food and probably eats his own weight in food every day. Of course, that means he must do a great deal of hunting, and he does.

"He makes tiny little paths under the fallen leaves and in swampy places—little tunnels through the moss. He is especially fond of old rotted stumps and logs and brush piles, for in such places he can find grubs and insects. At the same time he is well hidden. He is active by day and night, but in the daytime takes pains to keep out of the light. He prefers damp to dry places. In winter he tunnels about under the snow. In summer he uses the tunnels and runways of Meadow Mice and others when he can. He eats seeds and other vegetable food when he cannot find insects or flesh."

"How about his enemies?" asked Chatterer the Red Squirrel.

"He has plenty," replied Old Mother Nature, "but is not so much hunted as the members of the Mouse family. This is because he has a strong, unpleasant scent which makes him a poor meal for those at all particular about their food. Some of the Hawks and Owls appear not to mind this, and these are his worst enemies."

"Has he any near relatives?" asked Jumper the Hare.

"Several," was the prompt response. "Blarina the Short-tailed Shrew, also called Mole Shrew, is the best known. He is found everywhere, in forests, old pastures and along grassy banks, but seldom far from water. He prefers moist ground. He is much larger and thicker than Teeny Weeny and has a shorter tail. People often mistake him for Miner the Mole, because of the thick, fine fur which is much like Miner's and his habit of tunneling about just beneath the surface, but if they would look at his fore feet they would never make that mistake. They are small and like the feet of the Mouse family, not at all like Miner's big shovels. Moreover, he is smaller than Miner, and his tunnels are seldom in the earth but just under the leaves and grass.

"His food is much the same as that of Teeny Weeny—worms, insects, flesh when he can get it, and seeds. He is fond of beechnuts. He is quite equal to killing a Mouse of his own size or bigger and does not hesitate to do so when he gets the chance. He makes a soft, comfortable nest under a log or in a stump or in the ground and has from four to six babies at a time. Teeny Weeny sometimes has as many as ten. The senses of smell and hearing are very keen and make up for the lack of sight. His eyes, like those of other Shrews, are probably of use only in distinguishing light from darkness. His coat is dark brownish-gray.

"Another of the Shrew family is the Marsh Shrew, also called Water Shrew and Black-and white Shrew. He is longer than either of the others and, as you have guessed, is a lover of water. He is a good swimmer and gets much of his food in the water—water Beetles and grubs and perhaps Tadpoles and Minnows. Now who among you knows Miner the Mole?"

"I do. That is, I have seen him," replied Peter Rabbit.

"Very well, Peter, to-morrow morning we will see how much you know about Miner," replied Old Mother Nature.

CHAPTER XX
Four Busy Little Miners

Scampering along on his way to school and thinking of nothing so uninteresting as watching his steps, Peter Rabbit stubbed his toes. Yes, sir, Peter stubbed his toes. With a little exclamation of impatience he turned to see what he had stumbled over. It was a little ridge where the surface of the ground had been raised a trifle since Peter had passed that way the day before.

Peter chuckled. "Now isn't that funny?" he demanded of no one at all, for he was quite alone. Then he answered himself. "It certainly is," said he. "Here I am on my way to learn something about Miner the Mole, and I trip over one of the queer little ridges he is forever making. It wasn't here yesterday, so that means that he is at work right around here now. Hello, I thought so!"

Peter had been looking along that little ridge and had discovered that it ended only a short distance from him. Now as he looked at it again, he saw the flat surface of the ground at the end of the ridge rise as if being pushed up from beneath, and that little ridge became just so much longer. Peter understood perfectly. Out of sight beneath the surface Miner the Mole was at work. He was digging a tunnel, and that ridge was simply the roof to that tunnel. It was so near the surface of the ground that Miner simply pushed up the loose soil as he bored his way along, and this made the little ridge over which Peter had stumbled.

Peter watched a few minutes, then turned and scampered, lipperty-lipperty-lip, for the Green Forest. He arrived at school quite out of breath, the last one. Old Mother Nature was about to chide him for being late, but noticing his excitement, she changed her mind.

"Well, Peter," said she. "What is it now? Did you have a narrow escape on your way here?"

Peter shook his head. "No," he replied. "No, I didn't have a narrow escape, but I discovered something."

MINER THE MOLE. This shows how he uses his spade-like hands in digging.

THE STAR-NOSED MOLE. His nose is one of the oddest in the world.

Happy Jack Squirrel snickered. “Peter is always discovering something,” said he. “He is a great little discoverer. Probably he has just found out that the only way to get anywhere on time is to start soon enough.”

“No such thing!” declared Peter indignantly. “You—”

“Never mind him, Peter,” interrupted Old Mother Nature soothingly. “What was it you discovered?”

“That the very one we are to learn about is only a little way from here this very minute. Miner the Mole is at work on the Green Meadow; close to the edge of the Green Forest,” cried Peter eagerly. “I thought perhaps you would want to-”

“Have this morning’s lesson right there where we can at least see his works if not himself,” interrupted Old Mother Nature again. “That is fine, Peter. We will go over there at once. It is always better to see things than to merely hear about them.”

So Peter led the way to where he had stumbled over that little ridge on his way to school. It was longer than when he had left it, but even as the others crowded about to look, the earth was pushed up and it grew in length. Old Mother Nature stooped and made a little hole in that ridge. Then she put her lips close to it and commanded Miner to come out. She spoke softly, pleasantly, but in a way that left no doubt that she expected to be obeyed.

She was. Almost at once a queer, long, sharp nose was poked out of the little hole she had made, and a squeaky voice asked fretfully, “Do I have to come way out?”

“You certainly do,” replied Old Mother Nature. “I want some of your friends and neighbors to get a good look at you, and they certainly can’t do that with only that sharp nose of yours to be seen. Now scramble out here. No one will hurt you. I will keep you only a few minutes. Then you can go back to your everlasting digging. Out with you, now!”

While the others gathered in a little circle close about that hole there scrambled into view one of the queerest little fellows in all the Great World. Few of them had ever seen him close to before. He was a stout little fellow with the softest, thickest, gray coat imaginable. He was about six inches long and had a funny, short, pinkish-white, naked tail that at once reminded Peter of an Angleworm.

His head seemed to be set directly on his shoulders, so that there was no neck worth mentioning. His nose was long and sharp and extended far beyond his mouth. Neither ears nor eyes were to be seen.

Striped Chipmunk at once wanted to know how Miner could see. "He doesn't see as you do," replied Old Mother Nature. "He has very small eyes, tiny things, which you might find if you should part the fur around them, but they are of use only to distinguish light from darkness. Miner hasn't the least idea what any of you look like. You see, he spends his life under ground and of course has no use for eyes there. They would be a nuisance, for the dirt would be continually getting in them if they were any larger than they are or were not protected as they are. If you should feel of Miner's nose you would find it hard. That is because he uses it to bore with in the earth. Just notice those hands of his."

At once everybody looked at Miner's hands. No one ever had seen such hands before. The arms were short but looked very strong. The hands also were rather short, but what they lacked in length they made up in width and they were armed with long, stout claws. But the queer thing about them was the way he held them. He held them turned out. His hind feet were not much different from the hind feet of the Mouse family.

Miner was plainly uncomfortable. He wriggled about uneasily and it was very clear that he was there only because Old Mother Nature had commanded him to be there, and that the one thing he wanted most was to get back into his beloved ground. Old Mother Nature saw this and took pity on him. She picked him up and placed him on the ground where there was no opening near.

"Now, Miner," said she, "your friends and neighbors have had a good look at you, and I know just how uncomfortable you feel. There is but one thing more I'll ask of you. It is that you will show us how you can dig. Johnny Chuck thinks he is a pretty good digger. Just show him what you can do in that line."

Miner didn't wait to be told twice. The instant Old Mother Nature stopped speaking he began to push and bore into the earth with his sharp nose. One of those great, spadelike hands was slipped up past his face and the claws driven in beside his nose. Then it was swept back and the loosened earth with it. The other hand was used in the same way. It was quite plain to everybody why they were turned out in the way they were. There was nothing slow about the way Miner used that boring nose and those shoveling hands. Peter Rabbit had hardly time for half a dozen long breaths before Miner the Mole had disappeared.

"Some digging!" exclaimed Peter.

"Never again as long as I live will I boast of my digging," declared Johnny Chuck admiringly. From the point where Miner had entered the ground a little ridge was being pushed up, and they watched it grow surprisingly fast as the little worker under the sod pushed his tunnel along in the direction of his old tunnels. It was clear that he was in a hurry to get back where he could work in peace.

"What a queer life," exclaimed Happy Jack Squirrel. "He can't have much fun. I should think it would be awful living in the dark that way all the time."

"You forget that he cannot see as you can, and so prefers the dark," replied Old Mother Nature. "As for fun, he gets that in his work. He is called Miner because he lives in the ground and is always tunneling."

"What does he eat, the roots of plants?" asked Jumper the Hare.

Old Mother Nature shook her head. "A lot of people think that," said she, "and often Miner is charged with destroying growing crops, eating seed corn, etc. That is because his tunnels are found running along the rows of plants. The fact is Miner has simply been hunting for grubs and worms around the roots of those plants. He hasn't touched the plants at all. I suspect that Danny Meadow Mouse or one of his cousins could explain who ate the seed corn and the young plants. They are rather fond of using Miner's tunnels when he isn't about."

Danny hung his head and looked guilty, but didn't say anything. "The only harm Miner does is sometimes to tunnel so close to garden plants that he lets air in around the tender roots and they dry out," continued Old Mother Nature. "His food consists almost wholly of worms, grubs and insects, and he has to have a great many to keep him alive. That is why he is so active. Those tunnels of his which seem to be without any plan are made in his search for food. He is especially fond of Angleworms.

"As a matter of fact, he is a useful little fellow. The only time he becomes a nuisance to man is when he makes his little ridges across smooth lawns. Even then he pays for the trouble by destroying the grubs in the grass roots, grubs that in their turn would destroy the grass. When you see his ridges you may know that his food is close to the surface. When in dry or cold weather the worms go deep in the ground, Miner follows and then there is no trace of his tunnels on the surface.

"Night and day are all the same to him. He works and sleeps when he chooses. In winter he tunnels below the frost line. You all noticed how dense his fur is. That is so the sand cannot work down in it. His home is a snug nest of grass or leaves in a little chamber under the ground in which several tunnels offer easy means of escape in case of sudden danger."

"Has Miner any near relatives?" asked Peter Rabbit.

"Several," replied Old Mother Nature. "All are much alike in habits. One who lives a little farther north is called Brewer's Mole or the Hairytailed Mole. His tail is a little longer than Miner's and is covered with fine hair. The largest and handsomest member of the family is the Oregon Mole of the Northwest. His coat is very dark and his fur extremely fine. His ways are much the same as those of Miner whom you have just met, excepting that when he is tunneling deep in the ground he pushes the earth to the surface after the manner of Grubby Gopher, and his mounds become a nuisance to farmers. When he is tunneling just under the surface he makes ridges exactly like these of his eastern cousin.

"But the oddest member of the Mole family is the Star-nosed Mole. He looks much like Miner with the exception of his nose and tail. His nose has a fringe of little fleshy points, twenty-two of them, like a many-pointed star. From this he gets his name. His tail is a little longer than Miner's and is hairy. During the late fall and winter this becomes much enlarged.

"This funny little fellow with the star-like nose is especially fond of moist places, swamps, damp meadows, and the banks of streams. He is not at all afraid of the water and is a good swimmer. Sometimes he may be seen swimming under the ice in winter. He is seldom found where the earth is dry. For that matter, none of the family are found in those sections where there are long, dry periods and the earth becomes baked and hard.

"The fur of Miner and his cousins will lay in either direction, which keeps it smooth no matter whether the wearer is going forward or backward. Otherwise it would be badly mussed up most of the time. Altogether these little underground workers are most interesting little people when you know them. But that is something few people have a chance to do.

"Now just remember that the Shrews and the Moles belong to the order of Insectivora, meaning eaters of insects, and are the only two families in that order. And don't despise either of them, for they do a great deal of good in the Great World, more than some right here whom I might name, but will not. School is dismissed."

CHAPTER XXI
Flitter the Bat and His Family

In the dusk of early evening, as Peter Rabbit sat trying to make up his mind whether to spend that night at home in the dear Old Briar-patch with timid little Mrs. Peter or go over to the Green Forest in search of adventure, a very fine, squeaky voice which came right out of the air above him startled him for a moment.

"Better stay at home, Peter Rabbit. Better stay at home to-night," said the thin, squeaky voice.

"Hello, Flitter!" exclaimed Peter, as he stared up at a little dark form darting this way, twisting that way, now up, now down, almost brushing Peter's head and then flying so high he could hardly be seen. "Why should I stay at home?"

"Because I saw Old Man Coyote sneaking along the edge of the Green Forest, Reddy Fox is hunting on the Green Meadows, and Hooty the Owl is on watch in the Old Orchard," replied Flitter the Red Bat. "Of course it is no business of mine what you do, Peter Rabbit, but were I in your place I certainly would stay at home. Gracious! I'm glad I can go where I please when I please. You ought to fly, Peter. You ought to fly. There is nothing like it."

"I wish I could," sighed Peter.

"Well, don't say I didn't warn you," squeaked Flitter, and darted away in the direction of Farmer Brown's house. Peter wisely decided that the dear Old Briar-patch was the best place for him that night, so he remained at home, to the joy of timid little Mrs. Peter, and spent the night eating, dozing and wondering how it would seem to be able to fly like Flitter the Bat.

Flitter was still in his mind when he started for school the next morning, and by the time he got there he was bubbling over with curiosity and questions. He could hardly wait for school to be called to order. Old Mother Nature noticed how fidgety he was.

"What have you on your mind, Peter?" she asked.

"Didn't you tell us that the Shrew family and the Mole family are the only families in this country in the order of insect-eaters?" asked Peter.

"I certainly did," was the prompt reply. "Doesn't Flitter the Bat live on insects?" asked Peter.

Old Mother Nature nodded. "He does," said she. "In fact he lives altogether on insects."

"Then why isn't he a member of that order?" demanded Peter.

Old Mother Nature smiled, for she was pleased that Peter had thought of this. "That question does you credit, Peter," said she. "The reason is that he and his relatives are so very different from other animals that they have been placed in an order of their own. It is called the Chi-rop-ter-a, which means wing-handed. How many of you know Flitter the Bat?"

"I've often seen him," declared Jumper the Hare.

"So have I," said Chatterer the Red Squirrel. Each of the others said the same thing. There wasn't one who hadn't watched and envied Flitter darting about in the air just at dusk of early evening or as the Black Shadows were stealing away in the early morning. Old Mother Nature smiled.

"Seeing him isn't knowing him," said she. "Who is there who knows anything about him and his ways save that he flies at night and catches insects in the air?"

She waited a minute or two, but no one spoke. The fact is there was not one who really knew anything about Flitter. "It is one of the strange things of life," said she, "that people often know nothing about the neighbors whom they see every day. But in this case it is not to be wondered at. I suspect none of you has seen Flitter, excepting in the air, and then he moves so rapidly that there is no chance to get a good look at him. I think this is just the time and place for you to really make the acquaintance of Flitter the Red Bat."

She stepped over to a bush and parted the leaves. Hanging from a twig was what appeared at first glance to be a rumpled, reddish-brown dead leaf. She touched it lightly.

FLITTER THE BAT. This is the Red Bat, also called Tree Bat.

THE LITTLE BROWN BAT. He is about to catch a fly on the surface of the water.

At once it came to life, stirring uneasily. A thin, squeaky voice peevishly demanded to know what was wanted.

"You have some callers, a few of your friends who want to get really acquainted with you. Suppose you wake up for a few minutes," explained Old Mother Nature pleasantly.

Flitter, for that is just who it was, yawned once or twice sleepily, shook himself, then grinned down at the wondering faces of his friends crowded about just under him. "Hello, folks," said he in that thin, squeaky voice of his.

The sunlight fell full on him, but he seemed not to mind it in the least. In fact, he appeared to enjoy its warmth. He was hanging by his toes, head down, his wings folded. He was about four inches long, and his body was much like that of a Mouse. His fur was fine and thick, a beautiful orange-red. For his size his ears were large. Instead of the long head and sharp nose of the Mouse family, Flitter had a rather round head and blunt nose. Almost at once Peter Rabbit made a discovery. It was that Flitter possessed a pair of bright, little, snapping eyes and didn't seem in the least bothered by the bright light.

"Where did that saying 'blind as a Bat' ever come from?" demanded Peter.

Old Mother Nature laughed. "Goodness knows; I don't," said she. "There is nothing blind about Flitter. He sleeps through the day and does his hunting in the dusk of evening or early morning, but if he is disturbed and has to fly during the day, he has no trouble in seeing. Flitter, stretch out one of your wings so that everybody can see it."

Obediently Flitter stretched out one of his wings. Everybody gasped, for it was the first time any of them ever had seen one of those wings near enough to know just what it was like. Flitter's arm was long, especially from his elbow to his hand. But the surprising thing was the length of his three fingers. Each finger appeared to be about as long as the whole arm. From his shoulder a thin, rubbery skin was stretched to the ends of the long fingers, then across to the ankle of his hind foot on that side, and from there across to the tip of his tail. A little short thumb with a long, curved claw stuck up free from the edge of the wing.

"Now you can see just why he is called winghanded," explained Old Mother Nature, as Flitter folded the wing. In a minute he began to clean it. Everybody laughed, for it was funny to watch him. He would take the skin of the wing in his mouth and pull and stretch it as if it were rubber. He washed it with his tiny tongue. Then he washed his fur. You see, Flitter is very neat. With the little claw of his thumb he scratched his head and combed his hair. All the time he remained hanging head down, clinging to the twig with his toes.

"Where is Mrs. Flitter?" asked Old Mother Nature.

"Don't know," replied Flitter, beginning on the other wing. "She's quite equal to looking after herself, so I don't worry about her."

"Nor about your babies. Flitter, I'm ashamed of you. You are a poor kind of father," declared Old Mother Nature severely. "If you don't know where to find your family, I'll show you."

She stepped over to the very next tree, parted the leaves, and there, sure enough, hung Mrs. Flitter fast asleep. And clinging to her were three of the funniest babies in all the Great World! All were asleep, and Old Mother Nature didn't awaken them. As for Flitter, he seemed to take not the slightest interest in his family, but went right on with his toilet.

"Flitter the Red Bat is one of the best known of the whole family in this country," said Old Mother Nature, as they left Flitter to resume his nap. He is found from the East to the Far West, from ocean to ocean. Like the birds, he migrates when cold weather comes, returning in the early summer. Although, like all Bats, he sleeps all day as a rule, he doesn't mind the sunlight, as you have just seen for yourselves. Sometimes on dull, dark days he doesn't wait for evening, but flies in the afternoon. Usually he is the first of the Bat family to appear in the evening, often coming out while it is still light enough to show the color of his red coat. No other member of his family has a coat of this color.

"Some people call him the Tree Bat. After seeing him hanging over there I think you can guess why. He rarely goes to a cave for his daytime sleep, as most of his relatives do, but hangs by his toes from a twig of a tree or bush, frequently not far from the ground, just as he is right now.

"As all of you who have watched him know, Flitter is a swift flier. This is because his wings are long and narrow. They are made for speed. I want you to know that the Bats are among the most wonderful of all my little people. Few if any birds can equal them in the air because of their wonderful ability to twist and turn. They are masters of the art of flying. Moreover, they make no sound with their wings, something which only the Owls among birds can boast of.

"You all saw the three babies clinging to Mrs. Flitter. Most Bats have but two babies at a time, occasionally only one, but the Red Bat and his larger cousin, the Hoary Bat, have three or four. Mrs. Flitter carries her babies about with her until they are quite big. When they are too large to be carried she leaves them hanging in a tree while she hunts for her meals.

"Flitter has many cousins. One of these is the Little Brown Bat, one of the smallest members of the family and found all over the country. He is brown all over. He is sometimes called the Cave Bat, because whenever a cave is to be found he sleeps there. Sometimes great numbers of these little Bats are found crowded together in a big cave. When there is no cave handy, a barn or hollow tree is used. Often he will creep behind the closed blinds of a house to spend the day.

"Very like this little fellow in color is his cousin the Big Brown Bat, called the House Bat and the Carolina Bat. He is especially fond of the homes of men. He is a little bigger than the Red Bat. While the latter is one of the first Bats to appear in the evening, the former is one of the last, coming out only when it is quite dark. He also found all over the country.

"The Silvery Bat is of nearly the same size and in many places is more common than any its cousins. The fur is dark brown or black with white tips, especially in the young. From this it gets its name. One of the largest and handsomest of the Bat cousins, and one of the rarest is the Hoary Bat. His fur is a mixture of dark and light brown tipped with white. He is very handsome. His wings are very long and narrow and he is one of the most wonderful of all fliers. He is a lover of the Green Forest and does his hunting high above the tree-tops, making his appearance late in the evening. Like the Red Bat he spends the hours of daylight hanging in a tree.

"Down in the Southeast is a member of the family with ears so big that he is called the Big-eared Bat. He is a little chap, smaller than Little Brown Bat, and his ears are half as long his head and body together. What do you think of that? For his size he has the biggest ears of any animal in all this great country. A relative in the Southwest is the Big-eared Desert Bat.

"All members of the Bat family are drinkers and usually the first thing they do when they start out at dusk is to seek water. All live wholly on insects, and for this reason they are among the very best friends of man. They eat great numbers of Mosquitoes. They do no harm whatever, which is more than can be said for some of the rest of you little folks. Now who shall we learn about next?"

CHAPTER XXII
AN INDEPENDENT FAMILY

Just as Old Mother Nature asked who they should learn about next, Happy Jack Squirrel spied some one coming down the Lone Little Path. "See who's coming!" cried Happy Jack.

Everybody turned to look down the Lone Little Path. There, ambling along in the most matter-of-fact and unconcerned way imaginable, came a certain small person who was dressed wholly in black and white.

"Hello, Jimmy Skunk," cried Chatterer the Red Squirrel. "What are you doing over here in the Green Forest?" Jimmy Skunk looked up and grinned. It was a slow, good-natured grin. "Hello, everybody," said he. "I thought I would just amble over here and see your school. I suppose all you fellows are getting so wise that pretty soon you will think you know all there is to know. Have any of you seen any fat Beetles around here?"

Just then Jimmy noticed Old Mother Nature and hastened to bow his head in a funny way. "Please excuse me, Mother Nature," he said, "I thought school was over. I don't want to interrupt."

Old Mother Nature smiled. The fact is, Old Mother Nature is rather fond of Jimmy Skunk. "You aren't interrupting," said she. "The fact is, we had just ended the lesson about Flitter the Bat and his relatives, and were trying to decide who to study about next. I think you came along at just the right time. You belong to a large and rather important order, one that all these little folks here ought to know about. How many cousins have you, Jimmy?"

Jimmy Skunk looked a little surprised at the question. He scratched his head thoughtfully. "Let me see," said he, "I have several close cousins in the Skunk branch of the family, but I presume you want to know who my cousins are outside of the Skunk branch. They are Shadow the

Weasel, Billy Mink and Little Joe Otter. These are the only ones I can think of now."

"How about Digger the Badger?" asked Old Mother Nature.

A look of surprise swept over Jimmy Skunk's face. "Digger the Badger!" he exclaimed. "Digger the Badger is no cousin of mine!"

"Tut, tut, tut!" chided Old Mother Nature. "Tut, tut, tut, Jimmy Skunk! It is high time you came to school. Digger the Badger is just as much a cousin of yours as is Shadow the Weasel. You are members of the same order and it is a rather large order. It is called the Car-niv-o-ra, which means 'flesh-eating.' You are a member of the Marten or Weasel family, and that family is called the 'Mus-tel-i-dae.' Digger the Badger is also a member of that family. That means that you two are cousins. You and Digger and Glutton the Wolverine belong to the stout-bodied branch of the family. Billy Mink, Little Joe Otter, Shadow the Weasel, Pekan the Fisher and Spite the Marten belong to its slim-bodied branch. But all are members of the same family despite the difference in looks, and thus, of course, are cousins. Seeing that you are here, Jimmy, I think we will find out just how much these little folks know about you.

"Peter Rabbit, tell us what you know about Jimmy Skunk."

"I know one thing about him," declared Peter, "and that's that he is the most independent fellow in the world. He isn't afraid of anybody. I saw Buster Bear actually step out of his way the other day."

Jimmy Skunk grinned. "Buster always treats me very politely," said Jimmy.

"I have noticed that everybody does, even Farmer Brown's boy," spoke up Happy Jack Squirrel.

"It is easy enough to be independent when everybody is afraid of you," sputtered Chatterer the Red Squirrel.

"Just why is everybody afraid of Jimmy Skunk," asked Old Mother Nature.

"They are afraid of that little scent gun he carries,"

JIMMY SKUNK. The common Skunk is of considerable economic value as well as a valuable fur-bearer.

THE LITTLE SPOTTED SKUNK. A small cousin of Jimmy Skunk. Note the curious pattern of his markings.

spoke up Peter Rabbit. “I wish I had one just like it.”

Old Mother Nature shook her head. “It wouldn’t do, Peter, to trust you with a gun like Jimmy Skunk’s,” said she. “You are altogether too heedless and careless. If you had a scent gun like Jimmy’s, I am afraid there would be trouble in the Green Forest and on the Green Meadow all the time. I suspect that you would drive everybody else away. Jimmy is never heedless or careless. He never uses that little scent gun unless he is in real danger or thinks he is. Usually he is pretty sure that he is before he uses it. I’ll venture to say that not one of you has seen Jimmy use that little scent gun.”

Peter looked at Jumper the Hare. Jumper looked at Chatterer. Chatterer looked at Happy Jack. Happy Jack looked at Danny Meadow Mouse. Danny looked at Striped Chipmunk. Striped looked at Johnny Chuck. Johnny looked at Whitefoot the Wood Mouse. Then all looked at Old Mother Nature and shook their heads. “I thought as much,” said she. “Jimmy is wonderfully well armed, but for defense only. He never makes the mistake of misusing that little scent gun. But everybody knows he has it, so nobody interferes with him. Now, Peter, what more do you know about Jimmy?”

“He’s lazy,” replied Peter.

“I’m not lazy,” retorted Jimmy Skunk. “I’m no more lazy than you are. You call me lazy just because I don’t hurry. I don’t have to hurry, and I never can see any good in hurrying when one doesn’t have to.”

“That will do,” interposed Old Mother Nature. “Go on, Peter, with what you know about Jimmy.” “He is good-natured,” said Peter, and grinned at Jimmy.

Jimmy grinned back. “Thank you, Peter,” said he.

“He is one of the best-natured people I know,” continued Peter. “I guess it is a lucky thing for the rest of us that he is. I have noticed that fat people are usually good-natured, and Jimmy is nearly always fat. In fact, I don’t think I have seen him what you would call really thin excepting very early in the spring. He eats Beetles and grubs and Grasshoppers and Crickets and insects of all sorts. I am told that he steals eggs when he can find them."

"Yes, and he catches members of my family when he can," spoke up Danny Meadow Mouse. "I never feel safe with Jimmy Skunk very near."

Jimmy didn't look at all put out. "I might as well confess that tender Mouse is rather to my liking," said he, "and I might add that I also enjoy a Frog now and then, or a Lizard or a fish."

"Also you might mention that young birds don't come amiss when you can get them," spoke up Chatterer the Red Squirrel maliciously.

Jimmy looked up at Chatterer. "That's a case of the pot calling the kettle black," said he and Chatterer made a face at him. But Chatterer said nothing more, for he knew that all the others knew that what Jimmy said was true: Chatterer had robbed many a nest of young birds.

"Is that all you know about Jimmy?" asked Old Mother Nature of Peter.

"I guess it is," replied Peter, "excepting that he lives in a hole in the ground, and I seldom see him out in winter. I rather think he sleeps all winter, the same as Johnny Chuck does."

"You've got another think coming, Peter," said Jimmy. "I sleep a lot during the winter, but I don't go into winter quarters until well after snow comes, and I don't sleep the way Johnny Chuck does. Sometimes I go out in winter and hunt around a little."

"Do you dig your house?" asked Old Mother Nature.

Jimmy shook his head. "Not when I can help myself," said he, "It is too much work. If I have to I do, but I would much rather use one of Johnny Chuck's old houses. His houses suit me first rate."

"I want you all to look at Jimmy very closely," said Old Mother Nature. "You will notice that he is about the size of Black Pussy, the Cat from Farmer Brown's, and that his coat is black with broad white stripes. But not all Skunks are marked alike. I dare say that no two of Jimmy's children would be exactly alike. I suspect that one or more might be all black, with perhaps a little bit of white on the tail. Notice that Jimmy's front feet have long, sharp claws. He uses these to dig out grubs and insects in the ground, and for pulling over sticks and stones in his search for beetles. Also notice that he places his feet on the ground very much as does Buster Bear. That big, bushy tail of his is for the purpose of warning folks. Jimmy never shoots that little scent gun without first giving warning. When that tail of his begins to go up in the air, wise people watch out.

"A lot of people make the mistake of thinking that Jimmy Skunk and his family do a great deal of harm. The truth is, they do a great deal of good to man. Once in a while they will make the mistake of stealing Chickens or eggs, but it is only once in a while. They make up for all they take in this way by the pests they destroy. Jimmy and Mrs. Skunk have a large family each year, usually from six to ten. Mrs. Skunk usually is living by herself when the babies are born, but when they are big enough to walk their father rejoins the family, and you may see them almost any pleasant evening starting out together to hunt for Grasshoppers, Beetles and other things. Often the whole family remains together the whole winter, not breaking up until spring. Jimmy is one of the neatest of all my little people and takes the best of care of his handsome coat. He isn't afraid of water and can swim if it is necessary. He does most of his hunting at night, sleeping during the day. He is one of the few little wild people who haven't been driven away by man, and often makes his home close to man's home.

"Jimmy has own cousins in nearly all parts of this great country. Way down in the Southwest is one called the Hog-nosed Skunk, one of the largest of the family. He gets his name because of the shape of his nose and the fact that he roots in the ground the same as a hog. He is also called the Badger Skunk because of the big claws on his front feet and the fact that he is a great digger. His fur is not so fine as that of Jimmy Skunk, but is rather coarse and harsh. He is even more of an insect eater than is Jimmy.

"The smallest of Jimmy's own cousins is the Little Spotted Skunk. He is only about half as big as Jimmy, and his coat, instead of being striped with white like Jimmy's, is covered with irregular white lines and spots, making it appear very handsome. He lives in the southern half of the country and in habits is much like Jimmy, but he is much livelier. Occasionally he climbs low trees. Like Jimmy he eats almost anything he can find. And it goes without saying that, like Jimmy, he carries a little scent gun. By the way, Jimmy, what do you do when you are angry? Show us."

Jimmy began to growl, a queer-sounding little growl, and at the same time to stamp the ground with his front feet. Old Mother Nature laughed. "When you see Jimmy do that," said she, "it is best to pretend you don't see him and keep out of his way."

"Hasn't Jimmy any enemies at all?" asked Peter Rabbit.

"That depends on how hungry some folks get," replied Old Mother Nature. "Hooty the Owl doesn't seem to mind Jimmy's little scent gun, but this is the only one I can think of who doesn't. Some of the bigger animals might take him if they were starving, but even then I think they would think twice. Who knows where Digger the Badger is living?"

"I do," replied Peter Rabbit. "He is living out on the Green Meadows over near the Old Pasture."

"All right, Peter," replied Old Mother Nature, "suppose you run over and pay him a visit and to-morrow morning you can tell us about it."

BILLY MINK. He is equally at home on land or in the water.

SHADOW THE WEASEL. In his winter coat of white he is called the Ermina.

CHAPTER XXIII
Digger and His Cousin Glutton

"Well, Peter," said Old Mother Nature, "did you visit Digger the Badger yesterday?"

"Yes'm," replied Peter, "I visited him, but I didn't find out much. He's a regular old grouch. He isn't the least bit neighborly. It took me a long time to find him. He has more holes than anybody I ever knew, and I couldn't tell which one is his home. When I did find him, he gave me a terrible scare. I didn't see him until I was right on top of him, and if I hadn't jumped, and jumped quickly, I guess I wouldn't be here this morning. He was lying flat down in the grass and he was so very flat that I just didn't see him. When I told him that I wanted to know all about him and his ways, he replied that it was none of my business how he lived or what he did, and that was all I could get out of him.

"I sat around awhile and watched him, but he didn't do much except take a sun bath. He certainly is a queer-looking fellow to be a member of the Weasel family. There's nothing about him that looks like a Weasel, that I could see. Of course, he isn't as broad as he is long, but he looks almost that when he is lying flat down and that long hair of his is spread out on both sides. He really has a handsome coat when you come to look at it. It is silvery gray and silky looking. It seems to be parted right down the middle of his back. His tail is rather short, but stout and hairy. His head and face are really handsome. His cheeks, chin and a broad stripe from his nose right straight back over his head are white. On each cheek is a bar of black. The back part of each ear is black, and so are his feet. He has rather a sharp nose. Somehow when he is walking he makes me think of a little, flattened-out Bear with very short legs. And such claws as he has on his front feet! I don't know any one with such big strong claws for his size.

I guess that must be because he is such a digger."

"That's a very good guess, Peter," said Old Mother Nature. "Has any one here ever seen him dig?"

"I did once," replied Peter. "I happened to be over near where he lives when Farmer Brown's boy came along and surprised Digger some distance from one of his holes. Digger didn't try to get to one of those holes; he simply began to dig. My gracious, how the sand did fly! He was out of sight in the ground before Farmer Brown's boy could get to him. Johnny Chuck is pretty good at digging, but he simply isn't in the same class with Digger the Badger. No one is that I know of, unless it is Miner the Mole. I guess this is all I know about him, excepting that he is a great fighter. Once I saw him whip a dog almost twice his size. I never heard such hissing and snarling and growling. He wouldn't tell me anything about how he lives."

"Very good, Peter, very good," replied Old Mother Nature, "That's as much as I expected you would be able to find out. Digger is a queer fellow. His home is on the great plains and in the flat, open country of the Middle West and Far West, where Gophers and Ground Squirrels and Prairie Dogs live. They furnish him with the greater part of his food. All of them are good diggers, but they don't stand any chance when he sets out to dig them out.

"Digger spends most of his time under ground during daylight, seldom coming out except for a sun bath. But as soon as jolly, round, red Mr. Sun goes to bed for the night, Digger appears and travels about in search of a dinner. His legs are so short and he is so stout and heavy that he is slow and rather clumsy, but he makes up for that by his ability to dig. He doesn't expect to catch any one on the surface, unless he happens to surprise a Meadow Mouse within jumping distance. He goes hunting for the holes of Ground Squirrels and other burrowers, and when he finds one promptly digs. He eats Grasshoppers, Beetles and small Snakes, as well as such small animals as he catches. It was well for you, Peter, that you jumped when you did, for I suspect that Digger would have enjoyed a Rabbit dinner.

"Very little is known of Digger's family life, but he is a good husband. In winter he sleeps as Johnny Chuck does, coming out soon after the snow disappears in the spring. Of all my little people, none has greater courage. When he is cornered he will fight as long as there is a breath of life in him. His skin is very tough and he is further protected by his long hair. His teeth are sharp and strong and he can always give a good account of himself in a fight. He is afraid of no one of his own size.

"Man hunts him for his fur, but man is very stupid in many things and this is an example. You see, Digger is worth a great deal more alive than dead, because of the great number of destructive Rodents he kills. The only thing that can be brought against him is the number of holes he digs. Mr. and Mrs. Digger have two to five babies late in the spring or early in the summer. They are born under ground in a nest of grass. As you may guess just by looking at Digger, he is very strong. If he once gets well into the ground, a strong man pulling on his tail cannot budge him. As Peter has pointed out, he isn't at all sociable. Mr. and Mrs. Digger are quite satisfied to live by themselves and be left alone. So he is rarely seen in daytime, but probably is out oftener than is supposed. Peter has told how he nearly stepped on Digger before seeing him. It is Digger's wise habit to lie perfectly still until he is sure he has been seen, so people often pass him without seeing him at all, or if they see him they take him for a stone.

"While Digger the Badger is a lover of the open country and doesn't like the Green Forest at all he has a cousin who is found only in the Green Forest and usually very deep in the Green Forest at that. This is Glutton the Wolverine, the largest and ugliest member of the family. None of you have seen him, because he lives almost wholly in the great forests of the North. He hasn't a single friend that I know of, but that doesn't trouble him in the least.

"Glutton has several names. He is called 'Carcajou' in the Far North, and out in the Far West is often called 'Skunkbear.' The latter name probably is given him because in shape and color he looks a good deal as though he might be half Skunk and half Bear. He is about three feet long with a tail six inches long, and is thickset and heavy. His legs are short and very stout. His hair, including that on the tail, is long and shaggy. It is blackish-brown, becoming grayish on the upper part of his head and cheeks. His feet are black. When he walks he puts his feet flat on the ground as a Bear does.

"Being so short of leg and heavy of body, he is slow in his movements. But what he lacks in this respect he makes up in strength and cunning. You think Reddy Fox and Old Man Coyote are smart, but neither begins to be as smart as Glutton the Wolverine. He is a great traveler, and in the Far North where the greater part of the fur of the world is trapped, he is a pest to the trappers. He will follow a trapper all day long, keeping just out of sight. No matter how carefully a trapper hides a trap, Glutton will find it and steal the bait without getting caught. Sometimes he even tears up the traps and takes them off and hides them in the woods. If he comes on a trap in which some other animal has been caught, he will eat the animal. His strength is so great that often he will tear his way into the cabins of hunters while they are absent and then eat or destroy all their food. His appetite is tremendous, and it is because of this that he is called Glutton. What he cannot eat or take away, he covers with filth so that no other animal will touch it. He is of ugly disposition and is hated alike by the animals and by man. His fur is of considerable value, but he is hunted more for the purpose of getting rid of him than for his fur. Sometimes when caught in a trap he will pick it up and carry it for miles.

"Mrs. Glutton has two or three babies in the spring. They live in a cave, but if a cave cannot be found, they use a hole in the ground which Mrs. Glutton digs. It is usually well hidden and seldom has been found by man. Glutton will eat any kind of flesh and seems not to care whether it be freshly killed or so old that it is decayed. The only way that hunters can protect their supplies is by covering them with great logs. Even then Glutton will often tear the logs apart to get at the supplies. Because of his great cunning, the Indians think he is possessed of an evil spirit.

"I think this will do for to-day. To-morrow we will take up another branch of the family, some members of which all of you know. I wonder if it wouldn't be a good plan to have Shadow the Weasel here."

Such a look of dismay as swept over the faces of all those little people, with the exception of Jimmy Skunk and Prickly Porky! "If— if—if you please, I don't think I'll come to-morrow morning," said Danny Meadow Mouse.

"I—I—I think I shall be too busy at home and will have to miss that lesson," said Striped Chipmunk.

Old Mother Nature smiled. "Don't worry, little folks," said she. "You ought to know that if I had Shadow here I wouldn't let him hurt one of you. But I am afraid if he were here you would pay no attention to me, so I promise you that Shadow will not be anywhere near."

THE BLACK-FOOTED FERRET. Yap Yap the Prarie Dog fears no one more than this relative of Shadow the Weasel.

CHAPTER XXIV
SHADOW AND HIS FAMILY

Every one was on hand when school opened the next morning, despite the fear that the mere mention of Shadow the Weasel had aroused in all save Jimmy Skunk and Prickly Porky. You see, all felt they must be there so that they might learn all they possibly could about one they so feared. It might help them to escape should they discover Shadow hunting them sometime.

"Striped Chipmunk," said Old Mother Nature, "you know something about Shadow the Weasel, tell us what you know."

"I know I hate him!" declared Striped Chipmunk, and all the others nodded their heads in agreement. "I don't know a single good thing about him," he continued, "but I know plenty of bad things. He is the one enemy I fear more than any other because he is the one who can go wherever I can. Any hole I can get into he can. I've seen him just twice in my life, and I hope I may never see him again."

"What did he look like?" asked Old Mother Nature.

"Like a snake on legs," declared Striped Chipmunk. "Anyway, that is what he made me think of, because his body was so long and slim and he twisted and turned so easily. He was about as long as Chatterer the Red Squirrel but looked longer because of his slim body and long neck. He was brown above and white below. His front feet were white, and his hind feet rather whitish, but not clear white. His short, round tail was black at the end. Somehow his small head and sharp face made me think of a Snake. Ugh! I don't like to think about him!"

"I saw him once, and he wasn't brown at all. Striped Chipmunk is all wrong, excepting about the end of his tail," interrupted Jumper the Hare. "He was all white, every bit of him but the end of his tail, that was black."

"Striped Chipmunk is quite right and so are you,"

declared Old Mother Nature. "Striped Chipmunk saw him in summer and you saw him in winter. He changes his coat according to season, just as you do yourself, Jumper. In winter he is trapped for his fur and he isn't called Weasel then at all, but Ermine."

"Oh," said Jumper and looked as if he felt a wee bit foolish.

"What was he doing when you saw him?" asked Old Mother Nature, turning to Striped Chipmunk.

"Hunting," replied Striped Chipmunk, and shivered. "He was hunting me. He had found my tracks where I had been gathering beechnuts, and he was following them with his nose just the way Bowser the Hound follows Reddy Fox. I nearly died of fright when I saw him."

"You are lucky to be alive," declared Chatterer the Red Squirrel.

"I know it," replied Striped Chipmunk and shivered again. "I know it. I guess I wouldn't be if Reddy Fox hadn't happened along just then and frightened Shadow away. I've had a kindlier feeling for Reddy Fox ever since."

"I never ran harder in my life than the time I saw him," spoke up Jumper the Hare. "He was hunting me just the same way, running with his nose in the snow and following every twist and turn I had made. But for that black-tipped tail I wouldn't have seen him until too late."

"Pooh!" exclaimed Jimmy Skunk. "The idea of a big fellow like you running from such a little fellow as my Cousin Shadow!"

"I'm not ashamed of running," declared Jumper. "I may be ever so much bigger, but he is so quick I wouldn't stand the least chance in the world. When I suspect Shadow is about, I go somewhere else, the farther the better. If I could climb a tree like Chatterer, it would be different."

"No, it wouldn't!" interrupted Chatterer. "No, it wouldn't. That fellow can climb almost as well as I can. The only thing that saved me from him once was the fact that I could make a long jump from one tree to another and he couldn't. He had found a hole in a certain tree where I was living, and it was just luck that I wasn't at home when he called. I was just returning when he popped out. I ran for my life."

"He is the most awful fellow in all the Great World," declared Whitefoot the Wood Mouse.

Jimmy Skunk chuckled right out. "A lot you know about the Great World," he said. "Why, you are farther from home now than you've ever been in your life before, yet I could walk to it in a few minutes. How do you know Shadow is the most awful fellow in the Great World?"

"I just know, that's all," retorted Whitefoot in a very positive though squeaky voice. "He hunts and kills just for the love of it, and no one, no matter how big he is, can do anything more awful than that. I have a lot of enemies. Sometimes it seems as if almost every one of my neighbors is looking for a Mouse dinner. But all but Shadow the Weasel hunt me when they are hungry and need food. I can forgive them for that. Every one must eat to live. But Shadow hunts me even when his stomach is so full he cannot eat another mouthful. That fellow just loves to kill. He takes pleasure in it. That is what makes him so awful."

"Whitefoot is right," declared Old Mother Nature, and she spoke sadly. "If Shadow was as big as Buster Bear or Puma the Panther or even Tufty the Lynx, he would be the most terrible creature in all the Great World because of this awful desire to kill which fills him. He is hot-blooded, quick-tempered and fearless. Even when cornered by an enemy against whom he has no chance he will fight to the last gasp. I am sorry to say that there is no kindness nor gentleness in him towards any save his own family. Outside of that he hasn't a friend in the world, not one."

"Hasn't he any enemies?" asked Peter Rabbit.

"Oh, yes," replied Old Mother Nature. "Reddy Fox, Old Man Coyote, Hooty the Owl and various members of the Hawk family have to be watched for by him. But they do not worry him much. You see he moves so quickly, dodging out of sight in a flash, that whoever catches him must be quick indeed. Then, too, he is almost always close to good cover. He delights in old stone walls, stone piles, brush-grown fences, piles of rubbish and barns and old buildings, the places that Mice delight in. In such places there is always a hole to dart into in time of danger. He hunts whenever he feels like it, be it day or night, and often covers considerable ground, though nothing to compare with his big, brown, water-loving cousin, Billy Mink. It is because of his wonderful ability to disappear in an instant that he is called Shadow.

"Shadow is known as the Common Weasel, Short-tailed Weasel, Brown Weasel, Bonaparte Weasel and Ermine, and is found all over the forested parts of the northern part of the country. A little farther south in the East is a cousin very much like him called the New York Weasel. On the Great Plains of the West is a larger cousin with a longer tail called the Long-tailed Weasel, Large Ermine, or Yellow-bellied Weasel. His smallest cousin is the Least Weasel. The latter is not much longer than a Mouse. In winter he is all white, even the tip of his tail. In summer he is a purer white underneath than his larger cousins. All of the Weasels are alike in habits. When running they bound over the ground much as Peter Rabbit does.

"In that part of the West where Yap Yap the Prairie Dog lives is a relative called the Blackfooted Ferret who looks like a large Weasel. He is about the size of Billy Mink, but instead of the rich dark brown of Billy's coat his coat is a creamy yellow. His feet are black and so is the tip of his tail. His face is whitish with a dark band across the eyes. He is most frequently found in Prairie dog towns and lives largely on Yap Yap and his friends. His ways are those of Shadow and his cousins. There is no one Yap Yap fears quite as much.

"The one good thing Shadow the Weasel does is to kill Robber the Rat whenever they meet. Robber, as you know, is big and savage and always ready for a fight when cornered. But all the fight goes out of him when Shadow appears. Perhaps it is because he knows how hopeless it is. When Shadow finds a barn overrun with Rats he will sometimes stay until he has killed or driven out the last one. Then perhaps he spoils it all by killing a dozen Chickens in a night.

"It is a sad thing not to be able to speak well of any one, but Shadow the Weasel, like Robber the Rat, has by his ways made himself hated by all the little people of the Green Forest and the Green Meadows and by man. There is not one to say a good word for him. Now to-morrow we will meet on the bank of the Smiling Pool instead of here."

GLUTTON THE WOLVERINE. He is the largest member of the Weasel family.

PEKAN THE FISHER. One of the valuable fur-bearing animals.

CHAPTER XXV
TWO FAMOUS SWIMMERS

The bank of the Smiling Pool was a lovely place to hold school at that hour of the day, which you know was just after sun-up. Everybody who could get there was on hand, and there were several who had not been to school before. One of these was Grandfather Frog, who was sitting on his big, green, lily pad. Another was Jerry Muskrat, whose house was out in the Smiling Pool. Spotty the Turtle was also there, not to mention Longlegs the Heron. You see, they hadn't come to school but the school had come to them, for that is where they live or spend most of their time.

"Good morning, Jerry Muskrat," said Old Mother Nature pleasantly, as Jerry's brown head appeared in the Smiling Pool. "Have you seen anything of Billy Mink or Little Joe Otter?"

"Little Joe went down to the Big River last night," replied Jerry Muskrat. "I don't know when he is coming back, but I wouldn't be surprised to see him any minute. Billy Mink was here last evening and said he was going up the Laughing Brook fishing. He is likely to be back any time. One never can tell when that fellow will appear. He comes and goes continually. I don't believe he can keep still five minutes."

"Who is that can't keep still five minutes?" demanded a new voice, and there was Billy Mink himself just climbing out on the Big Rock.

"Jerry was speaking of you," replied Old Mother Nature. "This will be a good chance for you to show him that he is mistaken. I want you to stay here for a while and to stay right on the Big Rock. I may want to ask you a few questions."

Just then Billy Mink dived into the Smiling Pool, and a second later his brown head popped out of the water and in his mouth was a fat fish. He scrambled back on the Big Rock and looked at Old Mother Nature a bit fearfully as he laid the fish down.

"I—I didn't mean to disobey," he mumbled. "I saw that fish and dived for him before I thought. I hope you will forgive me, Mother Nature. I won't do it again."

"Acting before thinking gets people into trouble sometimes," replied Old Mother Nature. "However, I will forgive you this time. The fact is you have just shown your friends here something. Go ahead and eat that fish and be ready to answer questions."

As Billy Mink sat there on the Big Rock every one had a good look at him. One glance would tell any one that he was a cousin of Shadow the Weasel. He was much larger than Shadow, but of the same general shape, being long and slender. His coat was a beautiful dark brown, darkest on the back. His chin was white. His tail was round, covered with fairly long hair which was so dark as to be almost black. His face was like that of Shadow the Weasel. His legs were rather short. As he sat eating that fish, his back was arched.

Old Mother Nature waited until he had finished his feast. "Now then, Billy," said she, "I want you to answer a few questions. Which do you like best, night or day?"

"It doesn't make any particular difference to me," replied Billy. "I just sleep when I feel like it, whether it be night or day, and then when I wake up I can hunt. It all depends on how I feel."

"When you go hunting, what do you hunt?" asked Old Mother Nature.

Billy grinned. "Anything that promises a good meal," said he. "I'm not very particular. A fat Mouse, a tender young Rabbit, a Chipmunk, a Frog, Tadpoles, Chickens, eggs, birds, fish; whatever happens to be easiest to get suits me. I am rather fond of fish, and that's one reason that I live along the Laughing Brook and around the Smiling Pool. But I like a change of fare, and so often I go hunting in the Green Forest. Sometimes I go up to Farmer Brown's for a Chicken. In the spring I hunt for nests of birds on the ground. In winter, if Peter Rabbit should happen along here when I was hungry, I might be tempted to sample Peter." Billy snapped his bright eyes wickedly and Peter shivered.

"If Jerry Muskrat were not my friend, I am afraid I might be tempted to sample him," continued Billy Mink.

"Pooh!" exclaimed Peter Rabbit. "You wouldn't dare tackle Jerry Muskrat."

"Wouldn't I?" replied Billy. "Just ask Jerry how he feels about it."

One look at Jerry's face showed everybody that Jerry, big as he was, was afraid of Billy Mink. "How do you hunt when you are on land?" asked Old Mother Nature.

"The way every good hunter should hunt, with eyes, nose and ears," replied Billy. "There may be folks with better ears than I've got, but I don't know who they are. I wouldn't swap noses with anybody. As for my eyes, well, they are plenty good enough for me."

"In other words, you hunt very much as does your cousin, Shadow the Weasel," said Old Mother Nature.

Billy nodded. "I suppose I do," said he, "but there's one thing he does which I don't do and that's hunt just for the love of killing.

"Once in a while I may kill more than I can eat, but I don't mean to. I hunt for food, while he hunts just for the love of killing."

"You all saw how Billy catches fish," said Old Mother Nature. "Now, Billy, I want you to swim over to the farther bank and show us how you run."

Billy obeyed. He slipped into the water, dived, swam under water for a distance, then swam with just his head out. When he reached the bank he climbed out and started along it. He went by a series of bounds, his back arched sharply between each leap. Then he disappeared before their very eyes, only to reappear as suddenly as he had gone. So quick were his movements that it was impossible for one of the little people watching to keep their eyes on him. It seemed sometimes as though he must have vanished into the air. Of course he didn't. He was simply showing them his wonderful ability to take advantage of every little stick, stone and bush.

"Billy is a great traveler," said Old Mother Nature. "He really loves to travel up and down the Laughing Brook, even for long distances. Wherever there is plenty of driftwood and rubbish, Billy is quite at home, being so slender he can slip under all kinds of places and into all sorts of holes. Quick as he is on land, he is not so quick as his Cousin Shadow; and good swimmer as he is, he isn't so good as his bigger cousin, Little Joe Otter. But being equally at home on land and in water, he has an advantage over his cousins. Billy is much hunted for his fur, and being hunted so much has made him very keen-witted. Mrs. Billy makes her home nest in a hole in the bank or under an old stump or under a pile of driftwood, and you may be sure it is well hidden. There the babies are born, and they stay with their mother all summer. Incidentally, Billy can climb readily. Billy is found all over this great country of ours. When he lives in the Far North his fur is finer and thicker than when he lives in the South. I wish Little Joe Otter were here. I hoped he would be."

"Here he comes now," cried Jerry Muskrat. "I rather expected he would be back." Jerry pointed towards where the Laughing Brook left the Smiling Pool on its way to the Big River. A brown head was moving rapidly towards them. There was no mistaking that head. It could belong to no one but Little Joe Otter. Straight on to the Big Rock he came, and climbed up. He was big, being one of the largest members of his family. He was more than three feet long. But no one looking at him could mistake him for any one but a member of the Weasel family. His legs were short, very short for the length of his body. His tail was fairly long and broad. His coat was a rich brown all over, a little lighter underneath than on the back.

"What's going on here?" asked Little Joe Otter, his eyes bright with interest.

"We are holding a session of school here today," explained Old Mother Nature. "And we were just hoping

SPITE THE MARTEN. He is found only in the great forests of the North.

LITTLE JOE OTTER. A famous fisherman and swimmer.

that you would appear. Hold up one of your feet and spread the toes, Little Joe."

Little Joe Otter obeyed, though there was a funny, puzzled look on his face. "Whyee!" exclaimed Peter Rabbit. "His toes are webbed like those of Paddy the Beaver!"

"Of course they're webbed," said Little Joe. "I never could swim the way I do if they weren't webbed."

"Can you swim better than Paddy the Beaver?" asked Peter.

"I should say I can. If I couldn't, I guess I would go hungry most of the time," replied Little Joe.

"Why should you go hungry? Paddy doesn't," retorted Peter.

"Paddy doesn't live on fish," replied Little Joe. "I do and that's the difference. I can catch a fish in a tail-end race, and that's going some."

"You might show us how you can swim," suggested Old Mother Nature.

Little Joe slipped into the water. The Smiling Pool was very still and the little people sitting on the bank could look right down and see nearly to the bottom. They saw Little Joe as he entered the water and then saw little more than a brown streak. A second later his head popped out on the other side of the Smiling Pool.

"Phew, I'm glad I'm not a fish!" exclaimed Peter and everybody laughed.

"You may well be glad," said Old Mother Nature. "You wouldn't stand much chance with Little Joe around. Like Billy Mink, Little Joe is a great traveler, especially up and down the Laughing Brook and the Big River. Sometimes he travels over land, but he is so heavy and his legs are so short that traveling on land is slow work. When he does cross from one stream or pond to another, he always picks out the smoothest going. Sometimes in winter he travels quite a bit. Then when he comes to a smooth hill, he slides down it on his stomach. By the way, Little Joe, haven't you a slippery slide somewhere around here?"

Little Joe nodded. "I've got one down the Laughing

Brook where the bank is steep," said he. "Mrs. Otter and I and our children slide every day."

"What do you mean by a slippery slide?" asked Happy Jack Squirrel, who was sitting in the Big Hickory-tree which grew on the bank of the Smiling Pool.

Old Mother Nature smiled. "Little Joe Otter and his family are quite as fond of play as any of my children," said she. "They get a lot of fun out of life. One of their ways of playing is to make a slippery slide where the bank is steep and the water deep. In winter it is made of snow, but in summer it is made of mud. There they slide down, splash into the water, then climb up the bank and do it all over again. In winter they make their slippery slide where the water doesn't freeze, and they get just as much fun in winter as they do in summer."

"I suppose that means that Little Joe doesn't sleep in winter as Johnny Chuck does," said Peter.

"I should say not," exclaimed Little Joe. "I like the winter, too. I have such a warm coat that I never get cold. There are always places where the water doesn't freeze. I can swim for long distances under ice and so I can always get plenty of food."

"Do you eat anything but fish?" asked Peter Rabbit.

"Oh, sometimes," replied Little Joe. "Once in a while I like a little fresh meat for a change, and sometimes when fish are scarce I eat Frogs, but I prefer fish, especially Salmon and Trout."

"How many babies do you have at a time?" asked Happy Jack Squirrel.

"Usually one to three," replied Little Joe, "and only one family a year. They are born in my comfortable house, which is a burrow in the bank. There Mrs. Otter makes a large, soft nest of leaves and grass. Now, if you don't mind, I think I will go on up the Laughing Brook. Mrs. Otter is waiting for me up there."

Old Mother Nature told Little Joe to go ahead. As he disappeared, she sighed. "I'm very fond of Little Joe Otter," said she, "and it distresses me greatly that he is hunted by man as he is. That fur coat of his is valuable, and man is forever hunting him for it. The Otters were once numerous all over this great country, but now they are very scarce, and I am afraid that the day isn't far away when there will be no Little Joe Otter. I think this will do for to-day. There are two other members of the Weasel family and these, like Little Joe and Billy Mink, are continually being hunted for their fur coats. I will tell you about them to-morrow."

CHAPTER XXVI
SPITE THE MARTEN AND PEKAN THE FISHER

"The two remaining members of the Weasel family none of you have ever seen," began Old Mother Nature, when she opened school at the old meeting place in the Green Forest the morning after their visit to the Smiling Pool. "You have never seen them because they live in the deep forests of the Far North. But were you living up there, you would know them, and the dread of them would seldom be out of your mind. One is called Spite the Marten and the other Pekan the Fisher.

"Spite the Marten is also called the Pine Marten and the American Sable, and he is one of the handsomest members of the Weasel family. Shadow the Weasel can climb, but he spends most of his time on the ground. Jimmy Skunk and Digger the Badger are not climbers at all. Little Joe Otter spends most of his time in the water. But Spite the Marten is a lover of the tree tops, and is quite as much at home there as Chatterer the Red Squirrel.

"When he is moving about in the trees, he looks much like a very large Squirrel, while on the ground he might be mistaken for a young Fox. His coat is a rich, dark, yellowish-brown, becoming almost black on the tail and legs. His throat usually is yellow, though sometimes it is almost white. The sides of his face are grayish, and his good-sized ears are grayish-white on the inside. His tail is about half as long as his body and is covered with long hair, but isn't bushy like a Squirrel's. While his general shape is that of Shadow the Weasel, his body is much heavier in proportion to his size.

"Chatterer, you and your Cousin Happy Jack may well be thankful that Spite the Marten doesn't live about here, for he is very fond of Squirrels and delights to hunt them. He can leap from tree to tree quite as easily as either of you, and the only possible means of escape for a Squirrel he is hunting is a hole too small for Spite to get into. No Squirrel is more graceful in the trees than is Spite.

"But he by no means confines himself to the trees. He is quite at home on the ground, and there he moves with much of the quickness of Shadow the Weasel. He delights to hunt Rabbits and he covers great distances, being even more of a traveller than Billy Mink. He doesn't kill for the love of killing, but merely for food. If he kills more than he can eat at a meal he buries it, and when he is hungry again he returns to it. Like all the other members of his family, he is a great hunter of Mice. Also he catches many birds, especially those birds which nest on the ground. Birds, eggs, Frogs, Toads, some insects and fish vary his bill of fare. But unlike his smaller cousins, he eats some other things besides flesh, including certain nuts, berries and honey.

"He isn't in the least social with his own kind but prefers to live alone and is always ready to fight if he meets another Marten. Being so great a traveler he has several dens. Mrs. Spite makes her nest of grass and moss in a hollow tree as a rule, occasionally in a hole in the ground. She has from one to five babies in the spring. Spite is not a good father, for he has nothing to do with his family.

"As I told you in the beginning he is found only in the great forests of the North. The darker and deeper they are, the better it suits him. His own cousin, Pekan the Fisher, and Tufty the Lynx, are probably the only natural enemies he has much cause to fear. His one great enemy is man. His coat is one of the most highly prized of all furs and he is persistently hunted and trapped. In fact, his coat is one of the chief prizes of the fur trappers.

"In this same deep, dark forest clear across the northern part of the country lives Pekan the Fisher, also called the Pennant Marten and Blackcat. He is larger and heavier than Spite the Marten and his coat is a brownish-black, light on the sides, and browner below. His nose, ears, feet and tail are black. He gets his name of Blackcat from his resemblance to a Cat with a bushy tail, though on the ground he looks more like a black Fox. Like his cousin, Spite the Marten, he lives in the pine and spruce forests and prefers to be near swamps. He is a splendid climber but spends quite as much time on the ground. However, he is even livelier in the trees than is Spite the Marten. Spite can catch a Squirrel in the tree tops, but Pekan can catch Spite, and often does. He isn't afraid of leaping to the ground from high up in a tree, and often when coming down a tree he comes down headfirst. He is very fond of hunting the cousins of Jumper the Hare and is so tireless that he can run them down. He is very clever and, like his cousin, Glutton the Wolverine, makes no end of trouble for trappers by stealing the baits from their traps.

"You all remember how frightened Prickly Porky was when I merely mentioned Pekan the Fisher. It was because Pekan is almost the only one Prickly Porky has reason to fear. If Pekan is hungry he doesn't hesitate to dine on Porcupine. He has learned how to turn a Porcupine on his back, and, as you have already found out, the under part of the Porcupine is unprotected.

"Just why Pekan should be called Fisher, I don't know. True, he eats fish when he can get them, but he isn't a water animal and doesn't go fishing as do Billy Mink and Little Joe Otter. His food is much the same as that of Spite the Marten. He is especially fond of Rabbit and Hare. He is so strong and savage that he can kill a Fox and often does. Bobby Coon is a good fighter and much bigger and heavier than Pekan, but he is no match for Pekan.

"Probably all of you have guessed that being a true Marten, Pekan's coat is highly prized by the fur trappers. He hates the presence of man and with good cause.

"Now this ends the Weasel family, but that's only one family of the order of Carnivora, or flesh eaters. There is one family you all know so well that I think we will take that up next. It is the family to which Reddy Fox and Old Man Coyote belong, and it is called the Dog family.

"To-morrow morning when you get here, I may have a surprise for you."

CHAPTER XXVII
Reddy Fox Joins the School

When school was called to order the following morning not one was missing. You see, with the exception of Jimmy Skunk and Prickly Porky, there was not one in whose life Reddy Fox did not have a most important part. Even Happy Jack the Gray Squirrel and Chatterer the Red Squirrel, tree folk though they were, had many times narrowly missed furnishing Reddy with a dinner. As for Johnny Chuck and Peter Rabbit and Jumper the Hare and Striped Chipmunk and Danny Meadow Mouse and Whitefoot the Wood Mouse, there were few hours of day or night when they did not have Reddy in mind, knowing that to forget him even for a few minutes might mean the end of them.

Just imagine the feelings of these little people when, just as they had comfortably seated themselves for the morning lesson, Reddy himself stepped out from behind a tree. Never before was a school so quickly broken up. In the winking of an eye Old Mother Nature was alone, save for Reddy Fox, Jimmy Skunk, and in the trees Prickly Porky the Porcupine and Happy Jack and Chatterer.

Reddy Fox looked as if he felt uncomfortable. "I didn't mean to break up your school," said he to Old Mother Nature. "I wouldn't have thought of coming if you hadn't sent for me."

Old Mother Nature smiled. "I didn't tell any one that I was going to send for you, Reddy," said she, "for I was afraid that if I did no one would come this morning. I promised them a surprise, but it is clear that no one guessed what that surprise was to be. Go over by that old stump near the Lone Little Path and sit there, Reddy."

Then Old Mother Nature called each of the little people by name, commanding each to return at once. She spoke sternly, very sternly indeed. One by one they appeared from all sorts of hiding places, glancing fearfully towards

REDDY FOX. The familiar Red Fox who holds his own against man.

THE GRAY FOX. In some places he is called the Tree Fox.

Reddy Fox, yet not daring to disobey Old Mother Nature.

When at last all were crowded about her as closely as they could get, Old Mother Nature spoke and this time her voice was soft. "I am ashamed of you," said she. "Truly I am ashamed of you. How could you think that I would allow any harm to come to you? Reddy Fox is here because I sent for him, but he is going to sit right where he is until I tell him he can go, and not one of you will be harmed by him. To begin with, I am going to tell you one or two facts about Reddy, and then I am going to find out just how much you have learned about him yourselves.

"It may seem queer to you that Reddy Fox belongs to the same family as Bowser the Hound, but it is true. Both are members of the Dog family and thus are quite closely related. Howler the Wolf and Old Man Coyote are also members of the family, so all are cousins. Look closely at Reddy and you will see at once that he looks very much like a small Dog with a beautiful red coat, white waistcoat, black feet and bushy tail. Now, Peter, you probably know as much about Reddy as any one here. At least you should. Tell us what you have learned in your efforts to keep out of his clutches."

Peter scratched a long ear thoughtfully and glanced sideways at Reddy Fox. "I certainly ought to know something about him," he began. "He was the very first person my mother warned me to watch for, because she said he was especially fond of young Rabbits and was the slyest, smartest and most to be feared of all my enemies. Since then I have found out that she knew just what she was talking about." Johnny Chuck, Danny Meadow Mouse and Whitefoot the Wood Mouse nodded as if they quite agreed. Then Peter continued, "Reddy lives chiefly by hunting, and in his turn he is hunted, so he needs to have sharp wits. When he isn't hunting me he is hunting Danny Meadow Mouse or Whitefoot or Striped Chipmunk or Mrs. Grouse, or Bob White, or is trying to steal one of Farmer Brown's Chickens, or is catching Frogs along the edge of the Smiling Pool, or grasshoppers out in the Green Meadows.

So far as I can make out, anything Reddy can catch furnishes him with food. I guess he doesn't eat anything but such things as these."

"Your guess is wrong, Peter," spoke up Reddy Fox, who had been listening with a grin on his crafty face. "I am rather fond of certain kinds of fruits. You didn't know that, did you, Peter?"

"No, I didn't," replied Peter. "I'm glad to know it. I think it is dreadful to live entirely by killing others."

"You might add," remarked Reddy, "that I like a meal of fish occasionally, and eggs are always welcome. I am not particular what I eat so long as I can get my stomach full."

"Reddy Fox hunts with ears, eyes and nose," continued Peter. "Many a time I've watched him listening for the squeak of Danny Meadow Mouse or watching for the grass to move and show where Danny was hiding; and many a time he has found my scent with his wonderful nose and followed me just as Bowser the Hound follows him. I guess there isn't much going on that Reddy's eyes, ears and nose don't tell him. But it is Reddy's quick wits that the rest of us fear most. We never know what new trick he will try. Lots of enemies are easy to fool, but Reddy isn't one of them. Sometimes I think he knows more about me than I know about myself. I guess it is just pure luck that he hasn't caught me with some of those smart tricks of his.

"Reddy hunts both day and night, but I think he prefers night. I guess it all depends on how hungry he is. More than once I've seen him bringing home a Chicken, but I am told that he is smart enough not to steal Chickens near his home, but always to go some distance to get them. Also I've been told that he is too clever to go to the same Chicken yard two nights in succession. So far as I know, he isn't afraid of any one except a hunter with a terrible gun. He doesn't seem to mind being chased by Bowser the Hound at all."

"I don't," spoke up Reddy. "I rather enjoy it. It gives me good exercise. Any time I can't fool Bowser by breaking my trail so he can't find it again, I deserve to be caught. I am not even so terribly afraid of a hunter with a gun. You see, usually I can guess what a hunter will do better than he can what I will do."

Old Mother Nature nodded. "That sounds like boasting," said she, "but it isn't. Reddy Fox is one of the few animals who has succeeded in holding his own against man, and he has done it simply by using his wits. There is no other animal as large as Reddy Fox who has succeeded as he has in living close to the homes of men. It is simply because he has made the most of the senses I have given him. He has learned to use his eyes, ears and nose at all times and to understand and make the most of the information they bring him. Reddy has always been hunted by man, and it is this very thing which has so sharpened his wits. It is seldom that he is guilty of making the same mistake twice. All of you little people fear Reddy, and I suspect some of you hate him. But always remember that he never kills for the love of killing, and only when he must have food. There would be something sadly missing in the Green Forest and on the Green Meadows were there no Reddy Fox. Reddy, where do you and Mrs. Reddy make your home? And how do you raise your babies?"

"This year our home is up in the Old Pasture," replied Reddy. "We have the nicest kind of a house dug in the ground underneath a big rock. It has only one entrance, but this is because there is no need of any other. No one could possibly dig us out there. Last year our home was on the Green Meadows and there were three doorways to that. The year before we dug our house in a gravelly bank just within the edge of the Green Forest. The babies are born in a comfortable bedroom deep underground. Sometimes we have a storeroom in addition to the bedroom; there Mrs. Reddy and I can keep food when there is more than can be eaten at one meal. When the babies are first born in the spring and Mrs. Reddy cannot leave them, I take food to her. When the youngsters are big enough to use their sharp little teeth, we take turns hunting food for them. Usually we hunt separately, but sometimes we hunt together. You know often two can do what one cannot. If Bowser the Hound happens to find the trail of Mrs. Reddy when there are babies at home, she leads him far away from our home. Then I join her, and take her place so that she can slip away and go back to the babies. Bowser never knows the difference.

"Our children are well trained if I do say it. We teach them how to hunt, how to fool their enemies, and all the tricks we have learned. No one has a better training than a young Fox."

"Here is a conundrum for you little folks," said Old Mother Nature. "When is a Red Fox not a Red Fox?" Everybody blinked. Most of them looked as if they thought Old Mother Nature must be joking. But suddenly Chatterer the Red Squirrel, whose wits are naturally quick, remembered how Old Mother Nature had told them that there were black Gray Squirrels. "When he is some other color," cried Chatterer.

"That's the answer," said Old Mother Nature. "Once in a while a pair of Red Foxes will have a baby who hasn't a red hair on him. He will be all black, with perhaps just the tip of his tail white. Or his fur will be all black just tipped with white. Then he is called a Black Fox or Silver Fox. He is still a Red Fox, yet there is nothing red about him. Sometimes the fur is only partly marked with black and then he is called a Cross Fox. A great many people have supposed that the Black or Silver Fox and the Cross Fox were distinct kinds. They are not. They are simply Red Foxes with different coats. The fur of the Silver Fox is considered by man to be one of the choicest of all furs and tremendous prices are paid for it. This means, of course, that a young Fox whose coat is black will need to be very smart indeed if he would live to old age, for once he has been seen by man he will be hunted unceasingly."

Reddy Fox had been listening intently and now Mother Nature noticed a worried look on his face. "What is it, Reddy?" said she. "You look anxious."

"I am anxious," said he. "What you have just said has

THE ARCTIC FOX. His coat is all white in the winter months.

THE BLUE FOX. This is really a color phase of the Arctic Fox.

worried me. You see, one of my cubs at home is all black. Now that I have learned that his fur is so valuable, Mrs. Reddy and I will have to take special pains to teach him all we know."

"I want you all to know that Reddy Fox and Mrs. Reddy mate for life," said Old Mother Nature. "Reddy is the best of fathers and the best of mates."

"There's one thing I do envy Reddy," spoke up Peter Rabbit, "and that is that big tail of his. It is a wonderful tail. I wish I had one like it."

How everybody laughed as they tried to picture Peter Rabbit with a big tail like that of Reddy Fox. "I am afraid you wouldn't get far if you had to carry that around," said Old Mother Nature. "Even Reddy finds it rather a burden in wet weather when it becomes heavy with water. That is one reason you do not find him abroad much when it is raining or in winter when the snow is soft and wet. Reddy Fox is at home all over the northern half of this country, and everywhere he is the same sly, clever fellow whom you all know so well.

"In the South and some parts of the East and West, Reddy has a cousin of about his own size whose coat is gray with red on the sides of his neck, ears and across his breast. The under part of his body is reddish, his throat and the middle of his breast are white. He is called the Gray Fox. He prefers the Green Forest to the open country, for he is not nearly as smart as his Cousin Reddy. He is, if anything, a better runner, but his wits are slower and he cannot so well hold his own against man. Instead of making his home in a hole in the ground, he usually chooses a hollow tree-trunk or hollow log. The babies are born in a nest of leaves in the bottom of a hollow tree. In some parts of the West this Fox is called the Tree Fox, because often he climbs up in low trees.

"The Gray Fox of the South is not the only cousin of Reddy's," continued Old Mother Nature. "In certain parts of the Great West, on the plains, lives one of the smallest of Reddy's cousins, called the Kit Fox or Swift. He is no larger than Black Pussy, Farmer Brown's Cat, and gets his name of Swift from his great speed in running. He is a prairie animal and lives in burrows in the ground as most prairie animals do. His back is of a grayish color, while his sides are yellowish red. Beneath he is white. The upper side of his tail is yellowish-gray, below it is yellowish, and the tip is black. In general appearance he is more like the Gray Fox than Reddy. He lacks the quick wit of Reddy Fox and is easily trapped.

"In the hot, dry regions of the Southwest, where the Kangaroo Rats and Pocket Mice live, is another cousin, closely related to the Kit Fox. This is called the Desert Fox. Like most of the little people who live on the desert, he is seldom seen by day. He is very swift of foot. He digs a burrow with several entrances and his food consists largely of Pocket Mice, Kangaroo Rats, Ground squirrels and such other small animals as are found in that part of the country. Like his cousin, the Kit Fox, he is not especially quick-witted. Neither the Kit Fox nor the Desert Fox are considered very valuable for their coats, and so are not hunted and trapped as much as are Reddy Fox and his two cousins of the Great North, the Arctic Fox and the Blue Fox.

"The Arctic, or White Fox, lives in the Far North, in the land of snow and ice. He is a little fellow, bigger than the Kit Fox, but only about two thirds the size of Reddy Fox, and very beautiful. Way up in the Far North his entire coat is snowy white the year round. The fur is long, very thick and soft. His tail is very large and handsome. When he lives a little farther south, he changes his coat in the summer to one of a bluish-brown. But just as soon as winter approaches, he resumes his white coat. The young are born in a burrow in the ground, if the parents happen to be living far enough south for the ground to be free of snow. In the Far North, their home is a burrow in a snow bank, and there the babies are born. The white coats of the Arctic Foxes, who live in a world of white, are of great help to them when hunting, or when trying to escape from enemies. It is difficult to see them against their white surroundings. In summer their food consists very largely of ducks and other wild fowl which nest in great numbers in the Far North. In the winter they hunt for Lemmings, Arctic Hares and a cousin of Mrs. Grouse called the Ptarmigan, who lives up there. They pick the bones left by Polar Bears and Wolves. Getting a living in winter is not easy, and so the Arctic Fox is a great traveler.

"The Blue Fox is really only a colored White Fox, just as the Black Fox is a black Red Fox, and his habits are, of course, just the same as the habits of the White Fox. There are some islands in the Far North, called the Pribilof Islands, and on them live many Blue Foxes. Both the White and the Blue Foxes are much hunted for their coats, which are considered very valuable by man. Certainly they are very beautiful. While these cousins of Reddy's are clever hunters they do not begin to be as quick-witted as Reddy, and so are much more easily trapped.

"Now I think this will do for Reddy Fox and his relatives. Reddy is going to stay right here with me, until the rest of you have had a chance to get home. After that you will have to watch out for yourselves as usual. Just remember that Reddy has become the quick-witted person he is because he has been so much hunted. If you are as smart as Reddy, you will understand that the more he hunts you, the quicker-witted you also will become. To-morrow we will take up Reddy's big cousins, the Wolves."

CHAPTER XXVIII
OLD MAN COYOTE AND HOWLER THE WOLF

"Of course, you all know to what branch of the Dog family Old Man Coyote belongs," said Old Mother Nature, and looked expectantly at the circle of little folks gathered around her. No one answered. "Well, well, well!" exclaimed Old Mother Nature, "I am surprised. I am very much surprised. I supposed that all of you knew that Old Man Coyote is a member of the Wolf branch of the family."

"Do you mean that he is really a true Wolf?" asked Striped Chipmunk timidly.

"Of course," replied Old Mother Nature. "He is all Wolf and nothing but Wolf. He is the Prairie Wolf, so called because he is a lover of the great open plains and not of the deep forests like his big cousin, Howler the Timber Wolf. Reddy Fox is smart, but sometimes I believe Old Man Coyote is smarter. You have got to get up very early indeed to get ahead of Old Man Coyote.

"Old Man Coyote varies in size from not so very much bigger than Reddy Fox to almost the size of his big cousin, Howler the Timber Wolf. Also he varies in color from a general brownish-gray to a yellowish-brown, being whitish underneath. His face is rather longer than that of Reddy Fox. He has a brushy tail, but it is not as thick as Reddy's.

"In his habits, Old Man Coyote is much like Reddy, but being larger and stronger he is able to kill larger animals, and has won the hate of man by killing young Pigs, Lambs, newly born Calves and poultry. Because of this, he has been and is continually hunted and trapped. But like Reddy Fox the more he is hunted the smarter he becomes, and he is quite capable of taking care of himself. He is one of the swiftest of all runners. Many people think him cowardly because he is always ready to run away at the least hint of danger. He isn't cowardly, however; he is simply smart—too smart to run any unnecessary risk. Old Man Coyote

HOWLER THE WOLF. The Timber or Gray Wolf, so long dreaded by man.

OLD MAN COYOTE. The Prarie Wolf who is as clever as Reddy Fox.

believes absolutely in safety first, a very wise rule for everybody. The result is that he is seldom led into the mistake of simply thinking a thing is all right. He makes sure that it is all right. Because of this he is very hard to trap. No matter how hungry he may be, he will turn his back on a baited trap, even when the trap is so cunningly hidden that he cannot see it.

"Old Man Coyote is a good father and husband and a good provider for his family. He and Mrs. Coyote have a large family every year, sometimes as many as ten babies. Their home is in the ground and is very similar to that of Reddy Fox. They eat almost everything eatable, including such animals and birds as they can catch, Frogs, Toads, Snakes and insects, dead bodies they may find, and even some fruits. Mr. and Mrs. Coyote often hunt together. Sometimes, when the children are full-grown, they all hunt together. When they do this they can pull down Lightfoot the Deer.

"Old Man Coyote has one of the strangest voices to be heard anywhere, and he delights to use it, especially at night. It is like many voices shouting together, and one who hears it for the first time cannot believe that all that sound comes from one throat.

"His big cousin, Howler the Gray Wolf, sometimes called Timber Wolf— is found now only in the forests of the North and the mountains of the Great West. Once he roamed over the greater part of this great country. Howler is as keen-witted as, and perhaps keener-witted than, Reddy Fox or Old Man Coyote, and added to this he has great strength and courage. He is one of the most feared of all the people of the Green Forest. In summer when food is plentiful, Howler and Mrs. Wolf devote themselves to the bringing up of their family and are careful not to be overbold. But when winter comes, Howler and his friends get together and hunt in packs. With their wonderful noses they can follow Lightfoot the Deer and run him down. They kill Sheep and young Cattle. The harder the winter the bolder they become, and they have been known to attack man himself. In the Far North they grow especially large, and because of the scarcity of food there in winter, they become exceedingly fierce. They can go an astonishingly long time without food and still retain their strength. But hunger makes them merciless. They will not attack each other, but if one in the pack becomes injured, the others will turn upon him, and kill and eat him at once.

"Howler and Mrs. Wolf mate for life, and each is at all times loyal to the other. They are the best of parents, and the little Wolves are carefully trained in all that a Wolf should know. Always the hand of man has been against them, and this fact has developed their wits and cunning to a wonderful degree. Man in his effort to destroy them has used poison, cleverly hiding it in pieces of meat left where Howler and his friends could find them. Howler soon found out that there was something wrong with pieces of meat left about, and now it is seldom that any of his family come to harm in that way. He is equally cunning in discovering traps, even traps buried in one of his trails. Sometimes he will dig them up and spring them without being caught.

"When Wolves hunt in packs they have a leader, usually the strongest or the smartest among them, and this leader they obey. In all the great forests there is no more dreadful sound than the howling of a pack of wolves. There is something in it that strikes terror to the hearts of all who hear it.

"The color of Howler's coat usually is brownish-gray and that is why he is called the Gray Wolf; but sometimes it is almost black, and in the Far North it becomes snowy white. Howler is very closely related to the Dogs which men keep as pets. They are really first cousins. Few Dogs dare meet Howler in battle."

"My!" exclaimed Peter Rabbit, "I am glad Howler doesn't live around here."

"You well may be," said Old Mother Nature. "He would make just about one bite of you, Peter."

Peter shivered. "Are Old Man Coyote and Howler friends?" asked Peter.

"I wouldn't call them exactly friends," replied Old Mother Nature. "Old Man Coyote takes pains to keep out of Howler's way, but he is clever enough to know that when Howler has made a good kill there may be some left after Howler has filled his own stomach. So when Howler is hunting in Old Man Coyote's neighbor hood, the latter keeps an eye and ear open to what is going on. In the long-ago days when Thunderfoot the Bison was lord of the prairies, Howler's family lived on the prairies as well as in the forests, but now Howler sticks pretty closely to the forests and mountains, leaving the prairies and brushy plains to Old Man Coyote."

"All branches of the Dog family do one thing: they walk on their toes. They never put the whole foot down flat as does Buster Bear. And, as you have already discovered, all branches of the Dog family are very smart. They are intelligent. Hello, there is Black Pussy, the cat from Farmer Brown's, coming down the Lone Little Path! I suspect it will be well for some of you smallest ones to get out of sight before she arrives. She doesn't belong over here in the Green Forest, but she has a cousin who does, Yowler the Bob Cat. Shall I tell you about Yowler and his cousins tomorrow?"

"We'd love to have you!" cried Happy Jack, speaking for all. Then, as Black Pussy was drawing near, they separated and went their several ways.

CHAPTER XXIX
YOWLER AND HIS COUSIN TUFTY

Jumper the Hare arrived at school a little late and quite out of breath from hurrying. His big soft eyes were shining with excitement. "You look as though you had had an adventure, Jumper," said Old Mother Nature.

"I have," replied Jumper. "It is a wonder I am here at all; I came so near to furnishing Yowler the Bob Cat a breakfast that it makes me shiver just to think of it. I guess if I hadn't been thinking about him, he would have caught me."

"Tell us all about it," demanded Old Mother Nature.

"Seeing Black Pussy over here yesterday, and knowing that to-day's lesson was to be about Yowler, I couldn't get cats out of my mind all day yesterday," began Jumper. "Black Pussy doesn't worry me, but I must confess that if there is any one I fear, it is Yowler the Bob Cat. Just thinking about him make me nervous. The more I tried not to think about him, the more I did think about him, and the more I thought about him, the more nervous I got. Then just before dark, on the bank of the Laughing Brook, I found some tracks in the mud. Those tracks were almost round, and that fact was enough to tell me who had made them. They were Yowler's footprints, and they hadn't been made very long.

"Of course, seeing those footprints made me more nervous than ever, and every time I saw a leaf move I jumped inside. My heart felt as if it were up in my throat most of the time. I had a feeling that Yowler wasn't far away. I hate that Cat! I hate the way he hunts! He goes sneaking about, without making a sound, or else he lies in wait, ready to spring without warning on the first one who happens along. A fellow never knows where to watch out for Yowler.

"I spent nearly all night sitting under a little hemlock tree with branches very close to the ground. I sat there

TUFTY THE LYNX. This is the Canada Lynx, also called Lucivee.

YOWLER THE BOB CAT. The Bay Lynx or common Wild Cat.

because I didn't dare do anything else. As long as I stayed there I felt reasonably safe, because Yowler would have to find me, and to do that he would have to cross an open place where I could see him. I knew that if I went roaming about I might walk right into his clutches.

"It was lucky I had sense enough to stay there. You know the moon was very bright last night. It made that open place in front of where I was hiding almost as light as day. Once I closed my eyes for just a minute. When I opened them, there was Yowler sneaking across that open place. Where he had come from, I don't know. He hadn't made a sound. Not a leaf rustled under his big feet. Right in the middle of that open place, where the moonlight was brightest, he stopped to listen, and I simply held my breath."

"Tell us how he looked," prompted Old Mother Nature.

"He looked just like what he is—a big Cat with a short tail," replied Jumper. "Just to look at him any one would know he was own cousin to Black Pussy. He had a round head, rather long legs, and was about twice as big as Black Pussy. His feet looked big, even for him. On the tips of his ears were a few long black hairs. His coat was yellowish to reddish-brown, with dark spots on it. His chin and throat were white, and underneath he was white spotted with black. There were spots all down his legs. He didn't have enough of a tail to call it a tail. It was whitish on the under side and had black stripes on the upper side, and all the time he kept twitching it just the way Black Pussy twitches her tail when she is out hunting. All of a sudden he opened his mouth and gave such a yell that it is a wonder I didn't jump out of my skin. It frightened me so that I couldn't have moved if I had wanted to, which was a lucky thing for me. The instant he yelled he cocked his head on one side and listened. That yell must have wakened somebody and caused them to move, for Yowler turned suddenly and crept swiftly and without a sound out of sight. A minute later I heard a jump, and then I heard a fluttering. I think he caught one of the Grouse family."

"Yelling that way is one of Yowler's tricks," explained

Old Mother Nature. "He does it for the same reason Hooty the Owl hoots. He hopes that it will startle some sleeper so that they will move. If they do, his keen ears are sure to hear it. Was that all of your adventure, Jumper?"

"No," replied Jumper. "I remained right where I was for the rest of the night. Just as daylight was beginning to steal through the Green Forest, I decided that it was safe to leave my hiding place and come over here. Half-way here I stopped for a few minutes in a thick clump of ferns. I was just about to start on again when I caught sight of something moving just back of an old stump. It was that foolish looking tail of Yowler's. Had he kept it still I wouldn't have seen him at all; but he was twitching it back and forth. He was crouched down close to the ground with all four feet drawn close together under him. There he crouched, and there I sat for the longest time. I didn't move, and he didn't move, save that foolish looking tail of his. I had begun to think that I would have to stay in that clump of ferns all day when suddenly Yowler sprang like a flash. There was a little squeak, and then I saw Yowler trot away with a Mouse in his mouth. I guess he must have seen that Mouse go in a hole and knew that if he waited long enough it would come out again. As soon as Yowler disappeared I hurried over here. That's all."

"That was a splendid account of Yowler and his way of hunting," said Old Mother Nature. "He does most of his hunting in just that way, sneaking about on the chance of surprising a Rabbit, Bird or Mouse, or else patiently watching and waiting beside a hole in which he knows some one has taken refuge. He hunts in the Green Forest exactly as Black Pussy, Farmer Brown's Cat, hunts Mice in the barn or Birds in the Old Orchard. In the spring Yowler destroys many eggs and young birds, not only those found in nests on the ground, but also those in nests in trees, for he is a splendid climber.

"Yowler is found in nearly all of the swampy, brushy and wooded parts of the whole country, excepting in the great forests of the Far North, where his cousin Tufty the Lynx lives. Yowler is himself a Lynx, the Bay Lynx. In some places he is called simply Wild Cat. In others he is called the Catamount. He is not so fond of the thick forests as he is of swamps, brush-grown hillsides, old pastures and places where there are great masses of briars. Rocky ledges where there are caves in which to hide and plenty of brush also suit him. He is a coward, but when cornered will fight, though he will run from a little Dog half his size and take to a tree. In the South he is quite common and there often steals Chickens and Turkeys, even young Pigs. He prefers to hunt at night, but sometimes is seen in broad daylight. Mrs. Yowler's kittens are born in a cave or in a hollow tree. Despite the fact that he is an expert climber, Yowler spends most of his time on the ground and is one of the worst enemies of Rabbits, Mice, Squirrels and ground Birds.

"In the great forests of the Far North lives Yowler's cousin, Tufty the Canada Lynx, also called Loup Cervier and Lucivee. He is nearly a third larger than Yowler. From the tip of each ear long tufts of black hair stand up. On each side of his face is a ruff of long hair. His tail is even shorter than Yowler's, and the tip of it is always wholly black. His general color is gray, mottled with brown. His face ruff is white with black border. Yowler's feet are large, but Tufty's are immense for his size. This is because Tufty lives where the snow lies deep for many months, and these big, broad feet enable him to travel about on the snow without breaking through. He can travel with ease where Reddy Fox, not half his size and weight, would break through at every step. Tufty's ways are much like those of his cousin, Yowler, save that he is a dweller in the deep woods. Anything he can catch is food for Tufty, but his principal food is the Northern Hare. The color of his coat blends with the shadows so that he seems like a living shadow himself. In summer food is plentiful, and Tufty lives well, but in winter Tufty has hard work to get enough. Rarely does he know what a full stomach means then. Like Howler he can go a surprising length of time without food and still retain his strength. At that time of year he is a great traveler. He has to be, in order to live.

"There is no fiercer looking animal in all the Green Forest than Tufty the Lynx, but despite this he is, like most Cats, cowardly. Only when cornered will he fight. He is possessed of a lively curiosity, and often he will stealthily follow a hunter or trapper for miles. The fur of his coat is very long and handsome, and he is hunted and trapped for this. As he lives for the most part far from the homes of men, he does less damage to man than does his cousin, Yowler the Bob Cat. Tufty must depend wholly for his living on the little people of the Green Forest. Sometimes he will attack a Fox. The pretty little spotted babies of Lightfoot the Deer are victims whenever he can find them.

"The darker and deeper the Green Forest, the better Tufty likes it. He makes his den under great tangles of fallen trees or similar places. Mr. And Mrs. Tufty often hunt together, and in early winter the whole family often join in the hunt.

"Yowler and Tufty are the only members of the Cat family now found in the eastern part of the country. Formerly, their big cousin, Puma the Panther, lived in the East, but he has been so hunted by man that now he is found only in the mountains of the Far West and in a few of the wildest places in the South. I will tell you about him tomorrow."

PUMA THE PANTHER. This is the Mountain Lion or Cougar, next to the largest of the Cat family in America.

CHAPTER XXX
Some Big and Little Cat Cousins

"Puma the Panther," began Old Mother Nature, "is the largest member of the Cat family in this country, with the exception of one which is found only in the extreme Southwest. Puma is also called Mountain Lion, Cougar and Painter. You all know how Black Pussy looks. If Black Pussy could grow to be over eight feet long and be given a yellowish-brown coat, whitish underneath, she would look very much like Puma the Panther. Unlike Yowler the Bob Cat and Tufty the Lynx, Puma has a long tail—just such a round tail as Black Pussy has. Being so large, Puma is of great strength, and he has all the grace and quickness in movement of a true Cat. As I told you yesterday, there was a time when Puma lived in the East. In fact, he was once in nearly all parts of this great country where there were forests. But as the country became settled by man, Puma was driven out, and now his home is chiefly in the great mountains of the Far West.

"Being so big, he must have much food. Instead of depending for his living on small animals and birds, Puma hunts the large animals. He is so big and so strong that he can kill Lightfoot the Deer without trouble, and there is no one Lightfoot dreads more than Puma. He is especially fond of Horse flesh, and in certain sections where herds of Horses are pastured, he has killed so many young Horses that he has won the undying hate of man.

"Big as he is, he is a coward and will run from a barking Dog. When desperate with hunger, he has been known to attack man, but such occasions have been very, very rare. The fact is, he fears man and will slink away at his approach. Like the true Cat that he is, he is wonderfully soft-footed and, despite his great size, moves silently. He makes his home among the ledges high up in the mountains. At night he goes forth to hunt. Once in a while he is seen hunting in daytime, but not often. Sometimes he may be seen basking in the sun, high up on the ledges. He is a good climber, like most Cats. He never shows himself boldly, but slinks about through the forest and among the rocks, the picture of stealth. This habit has won for him another name—that of Sneak Cat. Sometimes he sneaks up on his prey to within jumping distance. Again he lies in wait beside a path which certain animals are in the habit of using. He is capable of leaping a long distance, and when he strikes his prey his great weight, added to the force of his spring, is almost certain to knock it down, even though it be much bigger than Puma himself.

"Men hunt him with Dogs, for as I have already told you he will run from a barking Dog. Usually he doesn't run far before taking to a tree. The hunters follow and shoot him there. Were it not that he can be hunted in this way with Dogs, he would have little to fear from man, for he is so keen of sight and hearing and can move so swiftly and silently, that it is rarely man can surprise him. Sometimes he will follow a man just as Tufty the Lynx does, but usually for the same reason—curiosity. Despite the fact that he is a sneak and coward, he is so big and fierce-looking that he is feared by most men. Only those who really know him do not fear him.

"There is one other member of the Cat family in all this great land larger than Puma, and this is Jaguar, also called El Tigre. He is found only in a small part of the extreme Southwest, for he really belongs in the hot country to the south of this. Not only is he the largest, but he is the handsomest of all the Cat family. His coat is a beautiful deep yellow, covered with spots and rosettes of black. Beneath he is white with large black spots. He also has a fairly long tail. He is thick and heavy, and is not as long as Puma, but is stouter and heavier. He can kill Horses, Mules and Cattle with ease, but of course the principal part of his food consists of the wild animals about him. He is so savage in appearance that the mere sight of him always awakens fear. His method of hunting is much the same as that of the

THE JAGUAR. The largest and handsomest of the cats of America.

other members of the Cat family. Most of his hunting is done at night. While Puma the panther sometimes screams, Jaguar roars, and it is a very terrifying sound. All the little people and most of the big ones within hearing shiver when they hear it. Jaguar's head is large and he is tremendously strong in the jaws. Occasionally Jaguar is all black instead of being yellow and spotted.

"In this same part of the great Southwest lives a smaller cousin named Ocelot, often called Tiger Cat. Ocelot is only a little bigger than Black Pussy, whom you all know, and in shape is very like her. He also has a lovely coat. It is yellow, not a deep, rich yellow like Jaguar's, but a light yellow, thickly covered with black spots. On his cheeks and the back of his neck are black lines, and his tail is ringed with black. He likes best country where the brush is very thick and thorny, for there he can hunt in safety, with little fear of being hunted by man. Because of his smaller size, he lives chiefly on small animals, birds and reptiles. He sometimes kills and eats big Snakes. When he happens to live near man, he robs the Hen roosts just as Yowler does. In all his ways he is like the other members of the Cat family.

"A neighbor of his in that same country is the queerest looking member of the Cat family. He is called the Jaguarundi Cat or Eyra. Sometimes he is dressed in dull gray and sometimes in rusty red. His body is shaped more like that of Little Joe Otter than of any one else, and he has short legs and a long tail. He is a little larger than Little Joe, and his head is rather small and somewhat flattened, not so round as the heads of most of the other members of the Cat family. He likes to be in the vicinity of water and is a good swimmer. Not very much is known by man about his habits, but he is a true Cat, and the habits of all Cats are much the same."

CHAPTER XXXI
Bobby Coon Arrives

Old Mother Nature was just about to open school when a slight noise up the Lone Little Path drew all eyes in that direction. There, shuffling down the Lone Little Path, was a queer looking fellow. No one needed more than one look at that funny, sharp, black and white face of his to recognize him.

"Bobby Coon!" shouted Peter Rabbit. "Are you coming to join our school, Bobby?"

Bobby shuffled along a little nearer, then sat up and blinked at them sleepily. No one needed to be told that Bobby had been out all night. He rubbed his eyes and yawned. "Hello, everybody," said he. "I wish I felt as bright and lively as all of you look. I'd like to join your school, but I'm afraid if I did I would go to sleep right in the middle of the lesson. I ought to have been home an hour ago. So I guess I'll have to be excused."

Old Mother Nature pointed an accusing finger at Bobby Coon. "Bobby," said she, "You've been getting in mischief. Now own up you've been stealing some of that sweet, milky corn from Farmer Brown's cornfield."

Bobby Coon hung his head. "I—I—I don't think it was stealing," he mumbled. "That corn just grows, and I don't see why I shouldn't have my share of it. I help myself to other things, so why shouldn't I help myself to that?"

"I'll tell you why," replied Old Mother Nature. "Farmer Brown planted that corn and took care of it. If he hadn't planted it, there wouldn't have been any corn there. That makes it his corn. If it grew wild, you would have a perfect right to it. As it is, you haven't any right to it at all. Now take my advice, Bobby, and keep away from that cornfield. If you don't, you will get in trouble. One of these fine nights Bowser the Hound will find you there and you will have to run for your life. Keep away from temptation."

THE RING-TAILED OR CIVET CAT. He is neither a Cat nor a Civet but a Bassaris.

"But that corn is so good," sighed Bobby Coon, smacking his lips. "There is nothing I like better than sweet, milky corn, and if I don't get it from Farmer Brown's cornfield, I can't get it at all, for it doesn't grow wild. He'll never miss the little I take."

Old Mother Nature shook her head and looked very grave. "Bobby," said she, "that is no excuse at all. Mark what I say: If you keep on you certainly will get in trouble. If you would be satisfied to take just an ear or two, I don't believe Farmer Brown would care, but you know very well that you spoil many times what you eat. You sample one ear, then think that probably the next ear will be better and sweeter and you try that. By the time you get through you have spoiled a lot, and eaten only a little. I think I'll punish you a little myself by keeping you here a while. If you think you can't keep awake, just go over and sit down there by Prickly Porky; he'll keep you awake."

"I—I think I can keep awake," stammered Bobby and opened his eyes very wide as if he were trying to stretch his eyelids so as to make them stay open.

"I'll help you by asking you a few questions," replied Old Mother Nature. "Who is it that people sometimes call you the little cousin of?"

Bobby grinned. "Buster Bear," said he.

"That's right," replied Old Mother Nature.

"Of course, being a Raccoon, you are not a Bear, but you are related to the Bear family. I want you all to notice Bobby's footprints over yonder. You will see that the print of his hind foot shows the whole foot, heels and toes, and is a lot like Buster Bear's footprint on a small scale. Bobby shuffles along in much the same way that Buster walks. No one ever mistakes Bobby Coon for any one else. There is no danger that any one ever will as long as he carries that big, bushy tail with its broad black and gray rings. There is only one other in all this great country with a tail so marked, and that is a relative of Bobby's of whom I will tell you later. And there is no other face like Bobby's with its black cheeks. You will notice that Bobby is rather small around the shoulders, but is big and heavy around the hips. That gives him a clumsy look, but he is anything but clumsy. Despite the fact that his legs are not very long Bobby is a very good runner. However, he doesn't do any running unless he has to. Bobby, where were you before you went over to Farmer Brown's cornfield?"

Once more Bobby hung his head. It was quite clear that Bobby didn't want to answer that question. But Old Mother Nature insisted, and finally Bobby blurted it out. "I was up to Farmer Brown's hen house," said he.

"What for?" asked Old Mother Nature.

"Oh, just to look around," replied Bobby.

"To look around for what?" insisted Old Mother Nature.

"Well," said Bobby, "I thought one of those Hens up there might have dropped an egg that she didn't really care about."

"Bobby," said Old Mother Nature sternly, "why don't you own up that you went over there to try to steal eggs? Or did you think you might catch a tender young Chicken? Where were you night before last?"

"Over at the Laughing Brook and the Smiling Pool," replied Bobby promptly, evidently glad the subject had been changed.

"Well, you didn't find sweet corn or eggs or Chickens over there, did you?" said Old Mother Nature.

"No, but I caught three of the sweetest tasting little fish in a little pool in the Laughing Brook, and I got some of the tenderest Clams I've ever eaten," replied Bobby, smacking his lips. "I raked them out of the mud and opened them. Down at the Smiling Pool I had a lot of fun catching young Frogs. I certainly do like Frogs. It is great sport to catch them, and they are fine eating."

"I suppose you have had an eye on the beech trees and the wild grape-vines," said Old Mother Nature slyly.

Bobby's face brightened. "Indeed I have," said he. "There will be splendid crops of beechnuts and grapes this fall. My, but they will taste good!"

BOBBY COON. The Raccoon has the neat habit of washing his food.

UNC' BILLY POSSUM. The Opossum is the only Marsupial in North America.

Old Mother Nature laughed. "There is small danger that you will go hungry," said she. "When you can't find enough to eat times must be very hard indeed. For the benefit of the others you might add that in addition to the things mentioned you eat other fruits, including berries, insects of various kinds, birds when you can catch them, Mice, Turtles, in fact almost anything that can be eaten. You are not at all fussy about the kind of food. But you have one habit in regard to your food which it would be well if some of these other little folks followed. Do you know what it is?"

Bobby shook his head. "No," said he, "not unless you mean the habit I have of washing my food. If there is any water near, I always like to take what I am going to eat over to it and wash it; somehow it tastes better."

"Just so," replied Old Mother Nature. "More than once I've seen you in the moonlight beside the Laughing Brook washing your food, and it has always pleased me, for there is nothing like cleanliness and neatness. Did you raise a family this year, Bobby?"

"Mrs. Coon did. We had four of the finest youngsters you have ever seen over in a certain big hollow tree. They are getting big and lively now, and go out with their mother every night. I do hope the hunters will leave them alone this fall. I hate to think of anything happening to them. If they can just get through the hunting season safely, I'll enjoy my winter sleep better, and I know Mrs. Coon will."

At this Johnny Chuck pricked up his ears. "Do you sleep all winter, Bobby?" he asked eagerly.

"Not all winter, but a good part of it," replied Bobby. "I don't turn in until the weather gets pretty cold, and it is hard to find anything to eat. But after the first snow I'm usually ready to sleep. Then I curl up in a warm bed of leaves in a certain big hollow tree, and don't care how cold or stormy the weather is. Sometimes I wake up once or twice, when the weather is mild, and take a little walk around for exercise. But I don't go far and soon return to sleep."

"What do you do when Bowser the Hound gets after you?" asked Peter Rabbit.

"Run till I get out of breath," replied Bobby. "And if by that time I haven't been able to fool him so that he loses my trail, I take to a tree. Thank goodness, he can't climb a tree. Sometimes I climb from the top of one tree into the top of another, and sometimes into a third and then a fourth, when they are near enough together. That fools the hunters, if they follow Bowser."

"Have you any relatives, Bobby?" asked Old Mother Nature.

"I didn't know I had until you mentioned that fellow with the ringed tail you said you would tell us about. I didn't know there was anybody with a tail like mine, and I would like to know about it," replied Bobby.

"He isn't exactly a Raccoon, but he is more nearly related to you than any one else," replied Old Mother Nature. "His tail shows that. Aside from this, he is nothing like you at all. He is called the Ring-tailed Cat. But he doesn't look any more like a Cat than he does like you, and he isn't related to the Cat family at all. He has several names. He is called the Bassaris, the Civet Cat, Ring-tailed Cat, Coon Cat and Cacomixtle. Instead of being thick and clumsy-looking, as is Bobby here, he is long and rather slender, with a yellowish-brown coat, somewhat grayish on the back and whitish underneath. His head is rather small, long and beautifully shaped. His ears are of good size and very pretty. In some ways he looks like Reddy Fox. But the really beautiful thing about him is his tail. It is nearly as long as his body, thick and beautifully marked with black and white bands.

"He is quick and graceful in his movements, and, like Bobby, prefers to be abroad at night. Also, like Bobby, he eats about everything that he can find—flesh, reptiles, fruit, nuts and insects. He lives in the Far Southwest, and also in some of the mountains of the Far West. Why he should be called Civet Cat is more than I can guess, for he is neither a Civet nor a Cat. He is very clever at catching Mice, and sometimes he is kept as a pet, just as Farmer Brown keeps Black Pussy, to catch the Mice about the homes of men.

"Now, Bobby, you can trot along home, and I hope all that green corn you have eaten will not give you the stomach ache. To-morrow we will see what we can find out about Buster Bear."

CHAPTER XXXII
Buster Bear Nearly Breaks Up School

"Has Buster Bear a tail?" asked Old Mother Nature, and her eyes twinkled.

"No," declared Whitefoot the Wood Mouse promptly.

"Yes," contradicted Chatterer the Red Squirrel.

"What do you say, Prickly Porky?" Old Mother Nature asked.

"I don't think he has any; if he has, I've never seen it," said Prickly Porky.

"That's because you've got poor eyes," spoke up Jumper the Hare. "He certainly has a tail. It isn't much of a one, but it is a tail. I know because I've seen it many times."

"Woof, woof," said a deep, rumbly, grumbly voice. "What's going on here? Who is it hasn't any tail?"

At the sound of that deep, rumbly, grumbly voice it looked for a few minutes as if school would be broken up for that day. There was the same mad scrambling to get away that there had been the morning Reddy Fox unexpectedly appeared. However, there was this difference: When Reddy appeared, most of the little people sought safe hiding places, but now they merely ran to safe distances, and there turned to stare with awe and great respect at the owner of that deep, rumbly, grumbly voice. It was great, big Buster Bear himself.

Buster stood up on his hind legs, like a man, and his small eyes, for they are small for his size, twinkled with fun as he looked around that awe filled circle. "Don't let me interrupt," said he. "I heard about this school and I thought I would just pay a friendly visit. There is nothing for you to fear. I have just had my breakfast and I couldn't eat another mouthful to save me, not even such a tender morsel as Whitefoot the Wood Mouse."

Whitefoot hurriedly ran a little farther away, and Buster Bear chuckled. Then he looked over at Old Mother Nature.

"Won't you tell them that I'm the best-natured and most harmless fellow in all the Great World?" he asked.

Old Mother Nature smiled. "That depends on the condition of your stomach," said she. "If it is as full as you say it is, and I know you wouldn't tell me an untruth, not even timid Whitefoot has anything to fear from you." Then she told all the little people to put aside their fears and return.

Buster, seeing that some of the more timid were still fearful, backed off a short distance and sat down on his haunches. "What was that about a tail I overheard as I came up?" he asked.

"It was a little discussion as to whether or not you have a tail," replied Old Mother Nature. "Some say you have, and some say you haven't. Whitefoot thinks you haven't."

Once more Buster Bear chuckled way down deep in his throat. "Whitefoot never in his life looked at me long enough to know whether I've got a tail or not," said he. "I never yet have seen him until now, when he wasn't running away as fast as his legs could take him. So with me always behind him, how could he tell whether or not I have a tail?"

"Well, have you?" demanded Peter Rabbit bluntly.

"What do you think?" asked Buster.

"I think you have," said Peter. "But if you have you are sitting down on it and I can't tell. It can't be much of a one, anyhow."

Again Buster chuckled. "Quite right, Peter; quite right," said he. "I've got a tail, but hardly enough of a one to really call it a tail."

As Buster sat there, every one had a splendid chance to see just how he looked. His coat was all black; in fact he was black all over, with the exception of his nose, which was brown. His fur was long and rather shaggy. His ears were round. His paws were big and armed with strong, wicked looking claws.

"You all see what a black coat Buster has," said Old Mother Nature. "Now I'm going to tell you something which may surprise you. Just as there are Red Foxes that are black, so there are Black Bears that are brown."

BUSTER BEAR THE BLACK BEAR. This is the most familiar of our American Bears. He is not always black, sometimes being light brown or cinnamon.

"What's that?" grunted Buster, with the funniest look of surprise on his face.

"It's a fact, Buster," said Old Mother Nature. "A great many of your family live out in the mountains of the Far West, and there quite often there will be one who is all brown. People used to think that these brown Bears were a different kind of Bear, and called them Cinnamon Bears. It was a long, long time before it was found out that those brown Bears are really black Bears. Sometimes one of the twin babies will be all black and the other all brown. Sometimes one of Buster's family will have a white spot on his breast. Buster's branch of the family is found in nearly all of the wooded parts of the entire country. In the Sunny South they live in the swamps and do not grow as big as in the North. Buster, there is a soft spot on the ground; I want you to walk across it so that these little folks can see your footprints."

Good-naturedly Buster dropped on all fours and walked across the soft spot. Right away every one understood why Old Mother Nature had asked Buster to do this. The prints of his hind feet were very like the prints of Farmer Brown's boy when barefooted, only of course very much larger. You see, they showed the print of the heel as well as the rest of the foot.

"You see," said Old Mother Nature, "Buster puts his whole foot on the ground, while all members of the Dog and Cat families walk wholly on their toes. Animals that put the whole foot down are called plantigrade. How big do you think Buster was when he was born?"

"Of course I'm only guessing," said Chatterer the Red Squirrel, "but he is such a big fellow that I think he must have been a bouncing big baby."

Old Mother Nature smiled. "I don't wonder you think so," said she. "The fact is, however, Buster was a very tiny and very helpless little chap. He was just about the size of one of Prickly Porky's babies. He was no bigger than a Rat. He was born in the middle of winter and didn't get his eyes open for forty days. It was two months before he poked his head outside the den in which he was born, to find out what the Great World was like. At that time he wasn't much bigger than Peter Rabbit, and he and his twin sister were as lively a pair of youngsters and as full of mischief as any Bears the Green Forest has ever seen. You might tell us, Buster, what you live on."

Buster's eyes snapped. "I live on anything I can eat, and I can eat most everything. I suppose a lot of people think I live almost wholly on the little people who are my neighbors, but that is a mistake. I do catch Mice when I am lucky enough to find them where I can dig them out, and they certainly are good eating."

At this Whitefoot the Wood Mouse and Danny Meadow Mouse hastily scurried farther away, and Buster's eyes twinkled with mischief. "Of course I don't mind a Rabbit either, if I am lucky enough to catch one," said he, and Peter Rabbit quickly backed off a few steps. "In fact I like meat of any kind," continued Buster. "But the greater part of my food isn't meat at all. In the spring I dig up roots of different kinds, and eat tender grass shoots and some bark and twigs from young trees. When the insects appear they help out wonderfully. I am very fond of Ants. I pull over all the old logs and tear to pieces all the old stumps I can find, and lick up the Ants and their eggs that I am almost sure to find there. Almost any kind of insect tastes good to me if there are enough of them. I love to find and dig open the nests of Wasps that make their homes in the ground, and of course I suppose you all know that there is nothing in the world I like better than honey. If I can find a Bee nest I am utterly happy. For the sake of the honey, I am perfectly willing to stand all the stinging the Bees can give me. I like fish and I love to hunt Frogs. When the berry season begins, I just feast. In the fall I get fat on beechnuts and acorns. The fact is, there isn't much I don't like."

"I've been told you sleep all winter," said Johnny Chuck.

"That depends on the winter," replied Buster Bear. "I don't go to sleep until I have to. I don't have to as long as I can find enough to eat. If the winter begins early, with bad weather, I make a comfortable bed of leaves in a cave or under a big pile of fallen trees or even in a hollow log, if I can find one big enough. Then I go to sleep for the rest of the winter. But if the winter is mild and open and there is a chance of finding anything to eat, I sleep only in the really bad weather."

"Do you try to get fat before going to sleep, the way I do?" asked Johnny Chuck.

Buster grinned. "Yes, Johnny, I try," said he, "and usually I succeed. You see, I need to be fat in order to keep warm and also to have something to live on in the spring, just the same as you do.

"I've been told that you can climb, but as I don't live in the Green Forest I have never seen you climb. I should think it would be slow work for such a big fellow as you to climb a tree," said Johnny Chuck.

Buster looked up at Happy Jack Squirrel and winked. Then he walked over to the tree in which Happy Jack was sitting, stood up and suddenly began to scramble up the tree. There was nothing slow about the way Buster Bear went up that tree. Happy Jack squealed with sudden fright and started for the top of that tree as only Happy Jack can climb. Then he made a flying jump to the next tree. Halfway up Buster stopped. Then he began to come down. He came down tail first. When he was within ten feet of the ground he simply let go and dropped.

"I did that just to show you how I get out of a tree when I am really in a hurry," explained Buster. "I don't climb trees much now unless it is for honey, but when I was a little fellow I used to love to climb trees."

Suddenly Buster sat up very straight and pointed his nose up in the wind. An anxious look crept into his face. He cocked his ears as if listening with all his might. That is just what he was doing. Presently he dropped down to all fours. "Excuse me," said he, "I think I had better be going. Farmer Brown is coming down the Lone Little Path."

Buster turned and disappeared at a speed that was simply astonishing in such a clumsy-looking fellow. Old

Mother Nature laughed. "Buster's eyes are not very good," said she, "but there is nothing the matter with his nose or with his ears. If Buster says that Farmer Brown is coming down the Lone Little Path, there is no doubt that he is, although he may be some distance away yet. Buster has been smart enough to learn that he has every reason to fear man, and he promptly takes himself out of the way at the first hint that man is near. It is a funny thing, but most men are as afraid of Buster as Buster is of them, and they haven't the least need of being afraid at all. Where man is concerned there isn't one of you little people more timid than Buster Bear. The faintest smell of man will make him run. If he should be wounded or cornered, he would fight. Mrs. Bear would fight to protect her babies, but these are the only conditions under which a Black Bear will face a man. You think Buster is big, and he is, but Buster has relatives very much bigger than he. He has one beside whom he would look actually small. I'll tell you a little about these cousins of Buster."

CHAPTER XXXIII
BUSTER BEAR'S BIG COUSINS

Buster Bear had been right about the coming of Farmer Brown. It was only a few minutes after Buster's disappearance that Farmer Brown's footsteps were heard coming down the Lone Little Path, and of course that ended school for that morning. But the next morning all were on hand again at sun-up, for every one wanted to hear about Buster Bear's big cousins.

"Way out in the mountains of the Far West, where Whistler the Marmot and Little Chief the Pika live, is a big cousin of Buster Bear," began Old Mother Nature. "He is Silvertip the Grizzly Bear, and in the past no animal in all this great country was so feared by man, as he. But times have changed, and Silvertip has been so hunted with terrible guns that he has learned to fear man quite as much as Buster does.

"He is larger than Buster and possessed of tremendous strength. Instead of a black coat, he has a coat which varies from yellowish-brown to almost black. The tips of the hairs usually are lighter, giving him a frosted appearance, and this is what has given him his name. His claws are longer and more curved than those of Buster; in fact those claws are so big that they look very terrible. Because they are so long, Silvertip cannot climb trees. But if they prevent him climbing trees they are the finest kind of tools for digging out Marmots and ground Squirrels. Even when Whistler the Marmot makes his home down in among the rocks, he is not safe. Silvertip's strength is so great that he can pull over and roll aside great rocks.

"He is a great traveler and covers a wide range of country in his search for food. Sometimes he visits the Cattle ranges and kills Cattle. So great is his strength that he can kill a Cow with ease. Clumsy looking as he is, he is a

SILVERTIP THE GRIZZLY BEAR. Famous for his fierce strength and fierceness he has been hunted until now. He must be protected to preserve the species.

BIGFOOT THE ALASKAN BROWN BEAR. Not only is he the largest of all Bears but he is the largest flesh eating mammal in the world.

very fast runner, and only a fast Horse can outrun him. Like Buster, he lives on anything he can find that is eatable. He has been so hunted by man that he has become very cunning, and in all the great mountains where he lives there is no one with quicker wits. At certain seasons of the year great numbers of a fish called Salmon come up the rivers in that country, and then Silvertip lives high. He watches beside a pool until a Salmon swims within reach; then, with a swift movement of one paw, he scoops the fish on to the bank. Or he finds a place where the water is so shallow that the fish have difficulty in getting across, and there he seizes them as they struggle up the river. In winter he sleeps just as Buster does, usually in a well-hidden cave.

"Mrs. Silvertip is a splendid mother. Usually the cubs, of which as a rule there are two, remain with her until they are a year old. Both Buster Bear and Silvertip have a queer habit of standing up against a tree and biting it as high up as they can reach. The next Bear who comes along that way sees the mark and makes his own on the same tree. Silvertip knows every inch of that part of the country in which he lives and always picks out the best way of getting from one place to another. He is one of the finest animals in this country, and it is a matter for sadness that his splendid race will soon come to an end unless man makes laws to protect him from the hunters. In very many places where he used to be found he lives no longer.

"Silvertip is not so good-natured as Buster, but all he asks is to be left alone. Of course when he turns Cattle killer he is getting into the worst possible kind of mischief and man cannot be blamed for hunting him. But it is only now and then that one of Silvertip's family turns Cattle killer. The others do no harm.

"I told you yesterday that Buster Bear has one cousin beside whom he would look small. This is Bigfoot the Alaska or Great Brown Bear, who lives in the extreme northwest part of the continent. Even Silvertip would look small beside him. He is a giant, the largest flesh-eating animal in all the great world. His coat is dark brown. When he stands up on his hind legs, he is almost half again as tall as a tall man. He stands very high at the shoulders and his head is very large. Like the other members of the Bear family, he eats all sorts of things. He hunts for Mice and other small animals, digs up roots, stuffs himself with berries, and at times grazes on a kind of wild grass, just as Cattle might do. He is a great fish eater, for fish are very plentiful in the streams in the country where he lives. Big as he is, he has learned to fear man just as Silvertip has. Occasionally when surprised he has been known to attack man and kill him, but as a rule he will run at the first hint of man's approach.

"The last of the Bear cousins is Snow King the Polar Bear. Snow King is king of the Frozen North. He lives in the region of snow and ice, and his coat is all white. He also is a big Bear, and of somewhat different shape from his cousins. He is longer, and has a much longer neck and a long head. His ears are rather small and close to his head. Snow King lives the year round where it would seem that no animal could live, and he manages to live well. Though his home is in the coldest part of the Great World, he does not mind the cold at all.

"More than any other member of the Bear family, Snow King is a flesh eater. This is because only in certain places, and then only for a few weeks in midsummer, is there any plant life. He is a great fisherman, and fish furnish him a great deal of his food. In that far northern country are great numbers of animals who live in the ocean, but come ashore to rest and bask in the sun, and to have their babies there. They are Seals, Sea Lions and Walruses. I will tell you about them later. On these Snow King depends for much of his food. He is himself a wonderful swimmer, and often swims far out in the icy water.

"Up there there are great fields of floating ice, and Snow King swims from one to another in search of Seals, for they often climb out on these ice fields, just as they do on shore. Sometimes Mrs. Bear takes her cubs for long swims. When they become tired, one will climb on her back, and the

SNOW KING THE POLAR BEAR. He is monarch of the Far North in the region of perpetual ice and snow.

other will seize her tail, so she will carry one and tow the other.

"Snow King's babies are born in a house of snow. Early in the winter Mrs. Bear finds a sheltered place where the snow will drift over her. There she goes to sleep, and the snow drifts and drifts over her until she is buried deep. You might think she would be cold, but she isn't, for the snow keeps her warm. Her breath melts a little hole up through the snow, so that she always has air. There the babies are born, and there they remain, just as Buster Bear's remain in their home, until they are big enough to follow their mother about. Then she breaks her way out in the spring, and leads her cubs forth to teach them how to take care of themselves. Snow King, himself, does not sleep through the winter, but roams about, just as in the summer.

"Snow King is fearless and has not yet learned to dread man, as have his cousins. He will not hesitate to attack man and is terrible to meet at close quarters. Because he lives in that far, cold country, he is not hunted as much as other bears are. Besides the Seals and fish, he sometimes catches an Arctic Hare. In the summer great numbers of Ducks and other sea birds nest in that far northern country, and their eggs and young add to Snow King's bill of fare. His white coat is so in keeping with his surroundings that it is of the greatest aid to him in his hunting. It is a very beautiful coat and makes him the most beautiful of all the Bear family.

"Now this is all about the Bears, and also it is all about the order of flesh eaters, or Carnivora. I think that next we will see what we can find out about a certain little friend of yours, who, though he eats flesh, is not a member of the flesh-eating order at all, but belongs to an order of which he is the only member in this country. I will leave you to guess who it is."

CHAPTER XXXIV
UNC' BILLY AND OLD MRS. POSSUM

All the way home from school Peter Rabbit did his best to think who it could be who ate flesh, yet wasn't a member of the order of flesh eaters. Every few hops he would stop to think, but all his stopping and all his thinking were in vain, and when he started for school the next morning he was as puzzled as ever. On his way through the Green Forest he passed a certain tree. He was just past and no more when a familiar voice hailed him.

"Morning, Bre'r Rabbit," said the voice. "What's yo' hurry?" Peter stopped abruptly and looked up in that tree. There, peering down at him from a hole high up in the trunk, was a sharp, whitish-gray face, with a pair of twinkling black eyes.

"Hello, Unc' Billy," cried Peter. "How are you and Ol' Mrs. Possum?"

"Po'ly, Peter, Po'ly. We-uns haven't had breakfast yet, so we-uns are feeling po'ly," replied Unc' Billy with a grin.

A sudden thought popped into Peter's head. "Unc' Billy," cried Peter excitedly, "are you a Carnivora?"

Unc' poked his head a little farther out and put his hand behind his ear as if he were a little hard of hearing. "What's that, Bre'r Rabbit? Am I a what?" he demanded.

"Are you a Carnivora?" repeated Peter.

"Ah reckons Ah might be if Ah knew what it was, but as long as Ah don't, Ah reckons I ain't," retorted Unc' Billy. "Ah reckons Ah'm just plain Possum. When Ah wants to be real uppity, Ah puts on an 'o.' Then Ah am Mister Opossum."

But Peter wasn't listening. The fact is, Peter had started lipperty-lipperty-lip for school, without even being polite enough to say good-by. He arrived at school quite out of breath. "I know!" he panted. "I know!"

"What do you know?" asked Old Mother Nature.

"I know who it is who eats flesh, yet doesn't belong to the order of flesh eaters. It's Unc' Billy Possum!" cried Peter.

"Right you are," replied Old Mother Nature. "However did you find it out?"

"I didn't exactly find it out; I guessed it," replied Peter. "On my way here I saw Unc' Billy, and it popped into my head right away that he was one we haven't heard about, and must be the one. But if he eats flesh, I don't see why he isn't a member of the order of flesh eaters."

"It is because he belongs to a group which has something which makes them entirely different from all other animals, and for this reason they have been given an order of their own," explained Old Mother Nature. "They belong to the order of Marsupials, which means pouched animals. It is because the mothers have big pockets in which they carry their babies. Old Mrs. Possum has just such a pocket."

"Of course," exclaimed Peter. "I've seen those babies poking their heads out of that pocket. They look too funny for anything."

"The Opossums are the only Marsupials in this country," continued Old Mother Nature. "Now have I made it quite clear why, although they eat flesh, Unc' Billy and Ol' Mrs. Possum are not members of the same big order as Buster Bear and the other flesh eaters?"

Everybody nodded. Just then Chatterer the Red Squirrel shouted, "Here comes Unc' Billy, Ol' Mrs. Possum and all the little Possums."

Sure enough, down the Lone Little Path came the Possum family, and a funny looking sight they were. Unc' Billy was whitish-gray, his face whiter than the rest of him. He looked as if he had just gotten out of bed and forgotten to brush his hair; it pointed every which way. His legs were dark, his feet black and his toes white. His ears were without any hair at all, and were black for the lower half, the rest being white. He had a long whitish tail without any hair on it. Altogether, with his sharp face and naked tail, he looked a great deal as though he might be a giant Rat.

But if Unc' Billy was a funny-looking fellow, Ol' Mrs. Possum was even more funny-looking. She seemed to have heads and tails all over her. You see, she had brought along her family, and Ol' Mrs. Possum is one of those who believe in large families. There were twelve youngsters, and they were exactly like their parents, only small. They were clinging all over Ol' Mrs. Possum. Some were on her back, some were clinging to her sides, and a couple were in the big pocket, where they had spent their babyhood.

"We—all done thought we'd come to school," explained Unc' Billy with a grin.

"I'm glad you did," replied Old Mother Nature. "You see, the rest of your friends here are a little curious about the Possum family."

Meanwhile Ol' Mrs. Possum was climbing a tree, and when she had reached a comfortable crotch the little Possums left her and began to play about in the tree. It was then that it appeared what handy things those naked little tails were. When the little Possums crawled out where the branches were small, they simply wrapped their tails around the twigs to keep from falling.

"My!" exclaimed Peter. "Those certainly are handy tails."

"Handiest tails ever was," declared Unc' Billy. "Don't know what Ah ever would do without mah tail."

"Suppose you climb a tree, Unc' Billy, and show your friends here how you manage to get the eggs from a nest that you cannot reach by crawling along the branch on which it is placed," said Old Mother Nature.

Unc' Billy grinned, and good-naturedly started up a tree. He crept out on a branch that overhung another branch. Way out where the branch was small crept Unc' Billy. Then he wrapped the end of his tail around the branch and swung himself off, keeping hold of the branch only with his tail and one hind foot. Then, stretching down full length, he could just reach the branch below him. "You see," he explained, "if there was a nest on this branch down here,

Ah could get those eggs without any trouble. Ah wish there was a nest. Just speaking of eggs makes mah mouth water." Again Unc' Billy grinned and then pulled himself back to the other branch.

Old Mother Nature shook her head reprovingly. "Unc' Billy," said she, "you are a bad old rascal to steal eggs. What's more, it doesn't matter to you much whether you find eggs or young birds in a nest. It is a wonder that between you and Chatterer the Red Squirrel any of the birds succeed in raising families around here. Have you visited Farmer Brown's hen house lately?"

Unc' Billy shook his head. "Not lately," said he; "Ah done got a dreadful scare the last time Ah was up there, and Ah reckons Ah'll stay away from there for a while."

"What else do you eat?" asked Old Mother Nature.

"Anything," replied Unc' Billy. "Ah reckons Ah ain't no ways particular—insects, roots, Frogs, Toads, small Snakes, Lizards, berries, fruits, nuts, young Rats and Mice, corn, any old meat that has been left lying around. Ah reckon Ah could find a meal most any time most anywhere."

"Do you always have as big a family as you have there?" asked Peter Rabbit.

"Not always," replied Unc' Billy. "But sometimes Mrs. Possum has to tote around a still bigger family. We believe in chillun and lots of them. We reckon on havin' two or three big families every year."

"Where is your home?" asked Johnny Chuck. "I know," said Peter Rabbit. "It's up in a big hollow tree."

Unc' Billy looked down at Peter. "'Tisn't at all necessary to tell anybody where that hollow tree is, Bre'r Rabbit," said he.

"Are Possums found anywhere except around here?" inquired Happy Jack.

"Yes, indeed," replied Old Mother Nature. "They are found all down through the Sunny South, and in the warmer parts of the Middle West. Unc' Billy and his relatives are not fond of cold weather. They prefer to be where they can be reasonably warm all the year round.

"Some folks think Unc' Billy isn't smart, but those folks don't know Unc' Billy. He learned a long time ago that he can't run as fast as some others, so he has learned to depend on his wits in time of danger. What do you think he does?"

"I know," cried Peter; "I saw him do it once. Farmer Brown's boy surprised Unc' Billy, and Unc' Billy just fell right over dead."

"Pooh! That's a story, Peter Rabbit. How could Unc' Billy have fallen over dead and be alive up in that tree this very minute?" cried Happy Jack.

"I didn't mean he was really dead, but that he looked as if he were dead," explained Peter. "And he did, too. He was the deadest looking thing I ever saw. I thought he was dead myself. I was watching from a bramble tangle where I was hiding, and I certainly thought the life had been scared right out of Unc' Billy. I guess Farmer Brown's boy thought so too. He picked Unc' Billy up by the tail, and looked him all over, and said, 'You poor little thing. I didn't mean to hurt you.' Unc' Billy didn't so much as wink an eye. Farmer Brown's boy went off up the path carrying Unc' Billy by the tail. By and by he laid Unc' Billy down on an old stump while he went to look at a nest of Blacky the Crow. When he came back Unc' Billy wasn't there. I never did see Unc' Billy hurry as he did the minute Farmer Brown's boy's back was turned. He came to life as suddenly as he had dropped dead."

"Very good, Peter," said Old Mother Nature. "Some other smart little people try that trick sometimes, but none of them can do it as well as Unc' Billy Possum. Pretending to be dead in order to remain alive is the cleverest thing Unc' Billy does. Now how about Lightfoot the Deer for the next lesson?"

"Splendid," cried all together and prepared to start for their homes.

LIGHTFOOT THE DEER. The Virginia or White-tailed Deer, known and loved by everybody.

FORKHORN THE MULE DEER. You may know him by the black tip of his tail, his mule-like ears and the forked tines of his antlers.

CHAPTER XXXV
LIGHTFOOT, BLACKTAIL AND FORKHORN

Of all the people who live in the Green Forest none is more admired than Lightfoot the Deer. So perhaps you can guess how delighted every one was when, just as the morning lesson was to begin, Lightfoot himself stepped daintily out from a thicket and bowed to Old Mother Nature.

"I heard," said he, "that my little friends here are to learn something about my family this morning, and thought you would not mind if I joined them."

"I should say not!" exclaimed Peter Rabbit forgetting that Lightfoot had spoken to Old Mother Nature.

All laughed, even Old Mother Nature. You see, Peter was so very much in earnest, and at the same time so excited, that it really was funny.

"Peter has spoken for all of us," said Old Mother Nature. "You are more than welcome, Lightfoot. I had intended to send for you, but it slipped my mind. I am delighted to have you here and I know that the others are. I suspect you will be most comfortable if you lie down, but before you do this I want everybody to have a good look at you. Just stand for a few minutes in that little open space where all can see you."

Lightfoot walked over to the open space where the sun fell full on him and there he stood, a picture of grace and beauty with just enough honest pride in his appearance to give him an air of noble dignity. There was more than one little gasp of admiration among his little neighbors.

"There," began Old Mother Nature, "is one of the most beautiful of all my children, and the knowledge that he is beautiful does not spoil him. Lightfoot belongs to the Deer family, as you all know, and this in turn is in the order called Ungulata, which means hoofed."

Peter Rabbit abruptly sat up, and his ears stood up like exclamation points. "Farmer Brown's cows have those funny feet called hoofs; are they related to Lightfoot?" he asked eagerly.

"They belong to another family, but it is in the same order. So they are distant cousins of Lightfoot," replied Old Mother Nature.

"And Farmer Brown's Pigs, what about them?" asked Chatterer the Red Squirrel. "They also belong to that order and so are related," explained Old Mother Nature.

"Huh!" exclaimed Chatterer. "If I were in Lightfoot's place I never, never would acknowledge any such homely, stupid creatures as those as relatives of mine."

"Don't forget that Prickly Porky the Porcupine and Robber the Rat are members of the same order to which you belong," retorted Old Mother Nature softly, and Chatterer hung his head. "Lightfoot," she continued, "is the White-tailed or Virginia Deer, and is in some ways the most beautiful of the Deer family. You have only to look at him to know that those slim legs of his are meant for speed. He can go very fast, but not for long distances without stopping. Like Peter Rabbit he is a jumper rather than a true runner, and travels with low bounds with occasional high ones when alarmed. He can make very long and high jumps, and this is one reason he prefers to live in the Green Forest where there are fallen trees and tangles of old logs. If frightened he can leap over them, whereas his enemies must crawl under or climb over or go around them. Ordinary fences, such as Farmer Brown has built around his fields, do not bother Lightfoot in the least. He can leap over them as easily as Peter Rabbit can jump over that little log he is sitting beside.

"Just now, because it is summer, Lightfoot's coat is decidedly reddish in color and very handsome. But in winter it is wholly different."

"I know," spoke up Chatterer the Red Squirrel. "It is gray then. I've often seen Lightfoot in winter, and there isn't a red hair on him at that season.

"Quite right," agreed Old Mother Nature. "His red coat

is for summer only. Notice that Lightfoot has a black nose. That is, the tip of it is black. Beneath his chin is a black spot. A band across his nose, the inside of each ear and a circle around each eye is whitish. His throat is white and he is white beneath. Now, Peter, you are so interested in tails, tell me without looking what color Lightfoot's tail is."

"White, snowy white," replied Peter promptly. "I suppose that is why he is called the White-tailed Deer."

"Huh!" grunted Johnny Chuck who happened to be sitting a little back of Lightfoot, "I don't call it white. It has a white edge, but mostly it is the color of his coat."

Now while Lightfoot had been standing there his tail had hung down, and it was as Johnny Chuck had said. But at Johnny's remark up flew Lightfoot's tail, showing only the under side. It was like a pointed white flag. With it held aloft that way, no one behind Lightfoot would suspect that his whole tail was not white.

"Notice how long and fluffy the hair on that tail is," said Old Mother Nature. "Mrs. Lightfoot's is just like it, and this makes it very easy for her babies to follow her in the dark. When Lightfoot is feeding or simply walking about he carries it down, but when he is frightened and bounds away, up goes that white flag. Now look at his horns. They are not true horns. The latter are hollow, while these are not. Farmer Brown's cows have horns. Lightfoot has antlers. Just remember that. The so-called horns of all the Deer family are antlers and are not hollow. Notice how Lightfoot's curve forward with the branches or tines on the back side."

Of course everybody looked at Lightfoot's crown as he held his head proudly. "What is the matter with them?" asked Whitefoot the Wood Mouse. "They look to me as if they are covered with fur. I always supposed them to be hard like bone."

"So they will be a month from now," explained Old Mother Nature, smiling down at Whitefoot. "That which you call fur will come off. He will rub it off against the trees until his antlers are polished, and there is not a trace of it left. You see Lightfoot has just grown that set this summer."

"Do you mean those antlers?" asked Danny Meadow Mouse, looking very much puzzled. "Didn't he have any before? How could things like those grow, anyway?"

"Don't you know that he loses his horns, I mean antlers, every year?" demanded Jumper the Hare. "I thought every one knew that. His old ones fell off late last winter. I know, for I saw him just afterward, and he looked sort of ashamed. Anyway, he didn't carry his head as proudly as he does now. He looked a lot like Mrs. Lightfoot; you know she hasn't any antlers."

"But how could hard, bony things like those grow?" persisted Danny Meadow Mouse.

"I think I will have to explain," said Old Mother Nature. "They were not hard and bony when they were growing. Just as soon as Lightfoot's old antlers dropped off, the new ones started. They sprouted out of his head just as plants sprout out of the ground, and they were soft and very tender and filled with blood, just as all parts of your body are. At first they were just two round knobs. Then these pushed out and grew and grew. Little knobs sprang out from them and grew to make the branches you see now. All the time they were protected by a furry skin which looks a great deal like what men call velvet. When Lightfoot's antlers are covered with this, they are said to be in the velvet state.

"When they had reached their full size they began to shrink and harden, so that now they are quite hard, and very soon that velvet will begin to come off. When they were growing they were so tender that Lightfoot didn't move about any more than was necessary and kept quite by himself. He was afraid of injuring those antlers. By the time cool weather comes, Lightfoot will be quite ready to use those sharp points on anybody who gets in his way.

"As Jumper has said, Mrs. Lightfoot has no antlers. Otherwise she looks much like Lightfoot, save that she is not quite as big. Have any of you ever seen her babies?"

"I have," declared Jumper, who, as you know, lives in the Green Forest just as Lightfoot does. "They are the dearest little things and look like their mother, only they have the loveliest spotted coats."

"That is to help them to remain unseen by their enemies," explained Old Mother Nature. When they lie down where the sun breaks through the trees and spots the ground with light they seem so much like their surroundings that unless they move they are not often seen even by the sharpest eyes that may pass close by. They lie with their little necks and heads stretched flat on the ground and do not move so much as a hair. You see, they usually are very obedient, and the first thing their mother teaches them is to keep perfectly still when she leaves them.

"When they are a few months old and able to care for themselves a little, the spots disappear. As a rule Mrs. Lightfoot has two babies each spring. Once in a while she has three, but two is the rule. She is a good mother and always on the watch for possible danger. While they are very small she keeps them hidden in the deepest thickets. By the way, do you know that Lightfoot and Mrs. Lightfoot are fine swimmers?"

Happy Jack Squirrel looked the surprise he felt. "I don't see how under the sun any one with little hoofed feet like Lightfoot's can swim," said he.

"Nevertheless, Lightfoot is a good swimmer and fond of the water," replied Old Mother Nature. "That is one way he has of escaping his enemies. When he is hard pressed by Wolves or Dogs he makes for the nearest water and plunges in. He does not hesitate to swim across a river or even a small lake.

"Lightfoot prefers the Green Forest where there are close thickets with here and there open places. He likes the edge of the Green Forest where he can come out in the open fields, yet be within a short distance of the protecting trees and bushes. He requires much water and so is usually found not far from a brook, pond or river. He has a favorite drinking place and goes to drink early in the morning and just at dusk. During the day he usually sleeps hidden away in a thicket or under a windfall, coming out late in the afternoon. He feeds mostly in the early evening. He eats grass and other plants, beechnuts and acorns, leaves and twigs of certain trees, lily pads in summer and, I am sorry to say, delights to get into Farmer Brown's garden, where almost every green thing tempts him.

"Like so many others he has a hard time in winter, particularly when the snows are deep. Then he and Mrs. Lightfoot and their children live in what is called a yard. Of course it isn't really a yard such as Farmer Brown has. It is simply a place where they keep the snow trodden down in paths which cross and cross, and is made where there is shelter and food. The food is chiefly twigs and leaves of evergreen trees. As the snow gets deeper and deeper they become prisoners in the yard until spring comes to melt the snow and set them free.

"Lightfoot depends for safety more on his nose and ears than on his eyes. His sense of smell is wonderful, and when he is moving about he usually goes up wind; that is, in the direction from which the wind is blowing. This is so that it will bring to him the scent of any enemy that may be ahead of him. He is very clever and cunning. Often before lying down to rest he goes back a short distance to a point where he can watch his trail, so that if any one is following it he will have warning.

"His greatest enemy is the hunter with his terrible gun. How any one can look into those great soft eyes of Lightfoot and then even think of trying to kill him is more than I can understand. Dogs are his next worst enemies when he lives near the homes of men. When he lives where Wolves, Panthers and Bears are found, he has to be always on the watch for them. Tufty the Lynx is ever on the watch for Lightfoot's babies.

"The White-tailed Deer is the most widely distributed of all the Deer family. He is found from the Sunny South to the great forests of the North—everywhere but in the vast open plains of the middle of this great country. That is, he used to be. In many places he has been so hunted by man that he has disappeared. When he lives in the Sunny South he never grows to be as big as when he lives in the North.

"In the great mountains of the Far West lives a cousin, Blacktail, also called Columbian Blacktailed Deer, and another cousin, Forkhorn the Mule Deer. Blacktail is nearly the size of Lightfoot. He is not quite so graceful, his ears are larger, being much like those of Forkhorn the Mule Deer, to whom he is closely related, and his tail is wholly black on the upper surface. It is from this he gets his name. His antlers vary, sometimes being much like those of Lightfoot and again like those of Forkhorn. He is a lover of dense forests and is not widely distributed. He is not nearly so smart as Lightfoot in outwitting hunters.

"Forkhorn the Mule Deer, sometimes called Jumping Deer, is larger than Lightfoot and much more heavily built. His big ears, much like those of a Mule, have won for him the name of Mule Deer. His face is a dull white with a black patch on the forehead and a black band under the chin. His tail is rather short and is not broad at the base like Lightfoot's. It is white with a black tip. Because of this he is often called Blacktailed Deer, but this is wrong because that name belongs to his cousin, the true Blacktail.

"Forkhorn's antlers are his glory. They are even finer than Lightfoot's. The prongs, or tines, are in pairs like the letter Y instead of in a row as are those of Lightfoot, and usually there are two pairs on each antler. Forkhorn prefers rough country and there he is very much at home, his powers of jumping enabling him to travel with ease where his enemies find it difficult to follow. Like Blacktail he is not nearly so clever as Lightfoot the White-tail and so is more easily killed by hunters.

"All these members of the Deer family belong to the round-horn branch, and are very much smaller than the members of the flat-horn branch. But there is one who in size makes all the others look small indeed. It is Bugler the Elk, or Wapiti, of whom I shall tell you to-morrow."

CHAPTER XXXVI
BUGLER, FLATHORNS AND WANDERHOOF

Lightfoot the Deer was the first one on hand the next morning. In fact, he arrived before sun-up and, lying down in a little thicket close at hand, made himself very comfortable to wait for the opening of school. You see, not for anything would he have missed that lesson about his big cousins. There the others found him when they arrived.

"The Deer family," began Old Mother Nature, "is divided into two branches—the round-horned and the flat-horned. I have told you about the round-horned Deer with the exception of the largest and noblest, Bugler the Elk. He is commonly called Elk, but his right name is Wapiti.

"Bugler is found only in the great mountains of the Far West, but once, before hunters with terrible guns came, Elk were found in nearly all parts of this country excepting the Far South and the Far North—even on the great plains. Now Bugler lives only in the forests of the great mountains."

"How big is he?" asked Lightfoot.

"So big that beside him you would look very small," replied Old Mother Nature. "Have you ever seen Farmer Brown's Horse?"

Lightfoot nodded. "Well, Bugler stands as high as that Horse," replied Old Mother Nature. "He isn't as heavy, for his body is of different shape, not so big around, but at that he weighs three times as much as you do. In summer his coat is a light yellowish-brown, becoming very dark on his neck and underneath. His legs are dark brown. The hair on his neck is long and coarse. His tail is very small, and around it is a large patch so light in color as to be almost whitish. In winter his coat becomes dark gray.

"Bugler's crowning glory are his antlers. They are very large and wide-spreading, sweeping backward and upward, the long prongs, or tines, curving upward from the front instead of from the back, as in the case of Lightfoot's

BUGLER THE ELK. To speak of him correctly you should call him Wapiti instead of Elk.

FLATHORNS THE MOOSE. He is the largest member of the deer family.

antlers. Above each eye is a long sharp prong. So big are these antlers that Bugler looks almost as if he were carrying a small, bare tree on his head.

"Big as these antlers are, they are grown in a few months for Bugler is like his small cousins in that he loses his antlers at the end of every winter and must grow a new pair. While they are growing, he hides in the wildest places he can find, high up on the mountains. Mrs. Bugler is at that time down in a valley with her baby or babies. Usually she has one, but sometimes twins. She has no antlers.

"In the fall, when his antlers have hardened, Bugler moves down to join his family. The bigger and stronger he is, the bigger his family is, for he has a number of wives and they all live together in a herd or band of which Bugler is lord and master. He is ready and eager to fight for them, and terrible battles take place when another disputes his leadership. At this season he has a habit of stretching his neck out and emitting a far-reaching trumpet-like sound from which he gets the name of Bugler. It is a warning that he is ready to fight.

"When the snows of winter come, many families get together and form great bands. Then they move down from the mountains in search of shelter and food. When a winter is very bad, many starve to death, for man has fenced in and made into farms much of the land where the elk once found ample food for winter.

"But big as is Bugler the Elk, there is a cousin who is bigger, the biggest of all the Deer family. It is Flathorns the Moose. As you must guess by his name he is a member of the flat-horned branch of the family. His antlers spread widely and are flattened instead of being round. From the edges of the flattened part many sharp points spring out.

"Flathorns, wearing his crown of great spreading antlers, is a noble appearing animal because of his great size, but when his antlers have dropped he is a homely fellow. Mrs. Flathorns, who has no antlers, is very homely. As I have said, Flathorns is the biggest member of the Deer family. He is quite as big as Farmer Brown's Horse and stands much higher at the shoulders. Indeed, his shoulders are so high that he has a decided hump there, for they are well above the line of his back. His neck is very short, large and thick, and his head is not at all like the heads of other members of the Deer family. Instead of the narrow, pointed face of other members of the Deer family, he has a broad, long face, rather more like that of a Horse. Towards the nose it humps up, and the great thick upper lip overhangs the lower one. His nose is very broad, and for his size his eyes are small. His ears are large.

"From his throat hangs a hairy fold of skin called a bell. He has a very short tail, so short that it is hardly noticeable. His legs are very long and rather large. His hoofs are large and rounded, more like those of Bossy the Cow than like those of Lightfoot the Deer. Seen at a little distance in the woods, he looks to be almost black, but really is for the most part dark brown. His legs are gray on the inside.

"Flathorns lives in the great northern forests clear across the country, and is especially fond of swampy places. He is fond of the water and is a good swimmer. In summer he delights to feed on the pads, stems and roots of water lilies, and his long legs enable him to wade out to get them. For the most part his food consists of leaves and tender twigs of young trees, such as striped maple, aspen, birch, hemlock, alder and willow. His great height enables him to reach the upper branches of young trees. When they are too tall for this, he straddles them and bends or breaks them down to get at the upper branches. His front teeth are big, broad and sharp-edged. With these he strips the bark from the larger branches. He also eats grass and moss. Because of his long legs and short neck he finds it easiest to kneel when feeding on the ground.

"Big as he is, he can steal through thick growth without making a sound. He does not jump like other Deer, but travels at an awkward trot which takes him over the ground very fast. In the winter when snow is deep, the Moose family lives in a yard such as I told you Lightfoot makes. The greatest enemy of Flathorns is the hunter, and from being much hunted Flathorns has learned to make the most of his ears, eyes and nose. He is very smart and not easily surprised. When wounded he will sometimes attack man, and occasionally when not wounded. Then he strikes with his sharp-edged front hoofs, and they are terrible weapons. Altogether he is a wonderful animal, and it is a matter for sorrow that man persists in hunting him merely to get his wonderful head.

"In parts of these same northern forests lives another big member of the Deer family, Wanderhoof the Woodland Caribou. He is bigger than Lightfoot the Deer, but smaller than Bugler the Elk, rather an awkward-looking fellow. His legs are quite long but stout. His neck is rather short, and instead of carrying his head proudly as does Lightfoot, he carries it stretched out before him or hanging low. The hair on the lower part of his neck is long.

"Wanderhoof wears a coat of brown. His neck being much lighter or almost gray. He has an undercoat which is very thick and woolly. In winter his whole coat becomes grayish and his neck white. Above each hoof is a band of white. His tail is very short, and white on the under side. His antlers are wonderful, being very long and both round and flat. That is, parts of them are round and parts flattened. They have more prongs than those of any other Deer.

"His hoofs are very large, deeply slit, and cup-shaped. When he walks they make a snapping or clicking sound. These big feet were given him for a purpose. He is very fond of boggy ground, and because of these big feet and the fact that the hoofs spread when he steps, he can walk safely where others would sink in. This is equally true in snow, when they serve as snowshoes. As a result he is not forced to live in yards as are Lightfoot and Flathorns when the snow is deep, but goes where he pleases.

"He is very fond of the water and delights to splash about in it, and is a splendid swimmer. His hair floats him so that when swimming he is higher out of water than any other member of the family. In winter he lives in the thickest parts of the forest among the hemlocks and spruces, and feeds on the mosses and lichens which grow on the trees. In summer he moves to the open, boggy ground around shallow lakes where moss covers the ground, and on this he lives.

"He is a great wanderer, hence his name Wanderhoof. Mrs. Caribou has antlers, wherein she differs from Mrs. Lightfoot, Mrs. Flathorns and Mrs. Bugler. Wanderhoof is fond of company and usually is found with many companions of his own kind. When they are moving from their summer home to their winter home, or back again, they often travel in very large bands.

"In the Far North beyond the great forests Wanderhoof has a cousin who looks very much like him, called the Barren Ground Caribou. The name comes from the fact that way up there little excepting moss grows, and on this the Caribou lives. In summer this Caribou is found almost up to the Arctic Ocean, moving southward in great herds as the cold weather approaches. No other animals of to-day get together in such great numbers. In the extreme North is another Caribou, called Peary's Caribou, whose coat is wholly white. The Caribou are close cousins of the Reindeer and look much like them.

"All male members of the smaller Deer are called bucks, the female members are called does, and the young are called fawns. All male members of the big Deer, such as Bugler the Elk, Flathorns the Moose and Wanderhoof the Caribou, are called bulls. The females are called cows and the young are called calves. All members of the Deer family, with the exception of the Barren Ground Caribou, are forest-loving animals and are seldom seen far from the sheltering woods.

"This, I think, will do for the Deer family. To-morrow I shall tell you about Thunderfoot the Bison, Fleetfoot the Antelope, and Longcoat the Musk Ox."

WANDERHOOF THE CARIBOU. This is the Woodland Caribou, a member of the Deer family closely related to the Reindeer.

CHAPTER XXXVII
THUNDERFOOT, FLEETFOOT AND LONGCOAT

"Who remembers the name of the order to which all members of the Deer family belong?" asked Old Mother Nature.

"I remember what it means, but not the name," spoke up Happy Jack Squirrel. "It means hoofed."

"It is Un—Un-Ungu—" began Peter Rabbit and then stopped. For the life of him he couldn't think of the rest.

"Ungulata," Old Mother Nature finished for him. "And Happy Jack has the meaning right. It is the order to which all hoofed animals belong. There are several families in the order, one of which you already have learned about—the Deer family. Now comes the family of Cattle and Sheep. It is called the Bovidae family, and the biggest and most important member is Thunderfoot the Bison, commonly called Buffalo.

"Thunderfoot is more closely related to Bossy, Farmer Brown's Cow, than are the members of the Deer family, for he has true horns, not antlers. These are hollow and are not dropped each year, but are carried through life. Mrs. Thunderfoot has them also. The horns grow out from the sides of the forehead and then curve upward and inward, and are smooth and sharp. They are never branched.

"Thunderfoot is a great, heavy fellow the size of Farmer Brown's Ox, and has a great hump on his shoulders. He carries his head low and from his throat hangs a great beard. His head is large and is so covered with thick, curly hair that it appears much larger than it really is. His tail is rather short and ends in a tassel of hair. The hair on his body and hind quarters is short and light brown, but on his shoulders and neck and his fore legs to the knees it is long and shaggy, dark brown above and almost black below."

"He must be a queer looking fellow," spoke up Chatterer the Red Squirrel.

"He is," replied Old Mother Nature. "The front half of him looks so much bigger than the rear half that it almost seems as if they didn't belong together."

"What does he eat?" asked Jumper the Hare.

"Grass," replied Old Mother Nature promptly. "He grazes just as does Bossy. When the weather becomes hot his thick coat, although much of it has been shed, becomes most uncomfortable. Also he is tormented by flies. Then he delights in rolling in mud until he is plastered with it from head to feet.

"Many years ago there were more Bison than any other large animal in this country, and they were found in nearly all parts of it. Some lived in the woods and were called Wood Buffaloes, but the greatest number lived on the great plains and prairies, where the grass was plentiful. I have told you about the great herd of Barren Ground Caribou, but this is nothing to the great herds of Bison that used to move north or south, according to the season, across the great prairies. In the fall they moved south. In the spring they moved north, following the new grass as it appeared. When they galloped, the noise of their feet was like thunder.

"But the hunters with terrible guns came and killed them for their skins, killed them by hundreds of thousands, and in just a few years those great herds became only a memory. Thunderfoot, once Lord of the Prairies, was driven out of all his great kingdom, and the Bison, from being the most numerous of all large animals, is to-day reduced to just a few hundreds, and most of these are kept in parks by man. Barely in time did man make laws to protect Thunderfoot. Without this protection he would not exist to-day.

"A close neighbor of Thunderfoot's in the days when he was Lord of the Prairies was Fleetfoot the Antelope. Fleetfoot is about the size of a small Deer, and in his graceful appearance reminds one of Lightfoot, for he has the same trim body and long slim legs. He is built for speed and looks it. From just a glance at him you would know him

FLEETFOOT THE ANTELOPE. Unless rigidly protected this beautiful animal will soon become extinct.

for a runner just as surely as a look at Jumper the Hare would tell you that he must travel in great bounds. The truth is, Fleetfoot is the fastest runner among all my children in this country. Not one can keep up with him in a race.

"Fleetfoot's coat is a light yellowish-brown on the back and white underneath. His forehead is brown and the sides of his face white. His throat and under side of his neck are white, crossed by two bands of brown. His hoofs, horns and eyes are black, and there is a black spot under each ear. Near the end of his nose he is also black, and down the back of his neck is a black line of stiff longer hairs. A large white patch surrounds his short tail. Who remembers what I told you about Antelope Jack, the big Jack Hare of the Southwest?"

"I do!" cried Peter Rabbit and Jumper the Hare together.

"What was it, Jumper?" asked Old Mother Nature.

"You said that he has a way of making the white of his sides seem to grow so that he seems almost all white, and can signal his friends in this way," replied Jumper.

"Quite right," replied Old Mother Nature. "I am glad to find that you remember so well. Fleetfoot does the same thing with this white patch around his tail. The hairs are quite long and he can make them spread out so that that white patch becomes much larger, and when he is running it can be seen flashing in the sun long after he is so far away that nothing else of him can be seen. His eyes are wonderfully keen, so by means of these white patches he and his friends can signal each other when they are far apart.

"Fleetfoot has true horns, but they are unlike any other horns in that they are shed every year, just like the antlers of the Deer family. They grow straight up just over the eyes, are rather short, and fork. One branch is much shorter than the other, and the longer one is turned over at the end like a hook. From these horns he gets the name of Pronghorn.

"When running from danger he carries his head low

and makes long leaps. When not frightened he trots and holds his head high and proudly. He prefers flat open country, and there is no more beautiful sight on all the great plains of the West than a band of Fleetfoot and his friends. He is social and likes the company of his own kind.

"The time was when these beautiful creatures were almost as numerous as the Bison, but like the latter they have been killed until now there is real danger that unless man protects them better than he is doing there will come a day when the last Antelope will be killed, and one of the most beautiful and interesting of all my children will be but a memory."

There was a note of great sadness in Old Mother Nature's voice. For a few minutes no one spoke. All were thinking of the terrible thing that had happened at the hands of man to the great hosts of two of the finest animals in all this great land, the Bison and Antelope, and there was bitterness in the heart of each one, for there was not one there who did not himself have cause to fear man.

Old Mother Nature was the first to break the silence. "Now," said she, "I will tell you of the oddest member of the Cattle and Sheep family. It is Longcoat the Musk Ox, and he appears to belong wholly neither to the Cattle nor the Sheep branch of the family, but to both. He connects the two branches in appearance, reminding one somewhat of a small Bison and at the same time having things about him very like a Sheep.

"Longcoat the Musk Ox lives in the Farthest North, the land of snow and ice. He has been found very near the Arctic Ocean, and how he finds enough to eat in the long winter is a mystery to those who know that snow-covered land. He is a heavily built, round-bodied animal with short, stout legs, shoulders so high that they form a hump, a low-hung head and sheeplike face, heavy horns which are flat and broad at the base and meet at the center of the forehead, sweeping down on each side of the head and then turning up in sharp points. His tail is so short that it is hidden in the long hair which covers him.

LONGCOAT THE MUSK OX. He is related to both cattle and sheep and his home is in the Arctic regions.

"This hair is so long that it hangs down on each side so that often it touches the snow and hides his legs nearly down to his feet. In color it is very dark-brown, almost black, and on his sides is straight. But on his shoulders it is curly. In the middle of the back is a patch of shorter dull-gray hair.

"Underneath this coat of long hair is another coat of woolly, fine light-brown hair, so close that neither cold nor rain can get through it. It is this warm coat that makes it possible for him to live in that terribly cold region. He is about twice as heavy as a big Deer. At times he gives off a musky odor, and it is from this that he gets his name of Musk Ox.

"Longcoat is seldom found alone, but usually with a band of his friends. This is partly for protection from his worst enemies, the Wolves. When the latter appear, Longcoat and his friends form a circle with their heads out, and it is only a desperately hungry Wolf that will try to break through that line of sharp-pointed horns.

"In rough, rocky country he is as sure-footed as a Sheep. In the short summer of that region he finds plenty to eat, but in winter he has to paw away the snow to get at the moss and other plants buried beneath it. Practically all other animals living so far North have white coats, but Longcoat retains his dark coat the year through.

"My, how time flies! This is all for to-day. To-morrow I will tell you of two wonderful mountain climbers who go with ease where even man cannot follow."

CHAPTER XXXVIII
Two Wonderful Mountain Climbers

"Peter, you have been up in the Old Pasture many times, so you must have seen the Sheep there," said Old Mother Nature, turning to Peter Rabbit.

"Certainly. Of course," replied Peter. "They seem to me rather stupid creatures. Anyway they look stupid."

"Then you know the leader of the flock, the big ram with curling horns," continued Old Mother Nature.

Peter nodded, and Old Mother Nature went on. "Just imagine him with a smooth coat of grayish-brown instead of a white woolly one, and immense curling horns many times larger than those he now has. Give him a large whitish or very light-yellowish patch around a very short tail. Then you will have a very good idea of one of those mountain climbers I promised to tell you about, one of the greatest mountain climbers in all the Great World—Bighorn the Mountain Sheep, also called Rocky Mountain Bighorn and Rocky Mountain Sheep.

"Bighorn is a true Sheep and lives high up among the rocks of the highest mountains of the Far West. Like all members of the order to which he belongs his feet are hoofed, but they are hoofs which never slip, and he delights to bound along the edges of great cliffs and in making his way up or down them where it looks as if it would be impossible for even Chatterer the Red Squirrel to find footing, to say nothing of such a big fellow as Bighorn.

"The mountains where he makes his home are so high that the tops of many of them are in the clouds and covered with snow even in summer. Above the line where trees can no longer grow Bighorn spends his summers, coming down to the lower hills only when the snow becomes so deep that he cannot paw down through it to get food. His eyesight is wonderful and from his high lookout he watches for enemies below, and small chance have they of approaching him from that direction.

BIGHORN THE MOUNTAIN SHEEP. His sure-footedness is the marvel or all who have seen him in his mountain home.

BILLY THE MOUNTAIN GOAT. His home is high in the great mountains of the Pacific coast.

"When alarmed he bounds away gracefully as if there were great springs in his legs, and his great curled horns are carried as easily as if they were nothing at all. Down rock slopes, so steep that a single misstep would mean a fall hundreds of feet, he bounds as swiftly and easily as Lightfoot the Deer bounds through the woods, leaping from one little jutting point of rock to another and landing securely as if he were on level ground. He climbs with equal ease where man would have to crawl and cling with fingers and toes, or give up altogether.

"Mrs. Bighorn does not have the great curling horns. Instead she is armed with short, sharp-pointed horns, like spikes. Her young are born in the highest, most inaccessible place she can find, and there they have little to fear save one enemy, King Eagle. Only such an enemy, one with wings, can reach them there. Bighorn and Mrs. Bighorn, because of their size, nothing to dread from these great birds, but helpless little lambs are continually in danger of furnishing King Eagle with the dinner he prizes.

"Only when driven to the lower slopes and hills by storms and snow does Bighorn have cause to fear four-footed enemies. Then Puma the Panther must be watched for, and lower down Howler the Wolf. But Bighorn's greatest enemy, and one he fears most, is the same one so many others have sad cause to fear—the hunter with his terrible gun. The terrible gun can kill where man himself cannot climb, and Bighorn has been persistently hunted for his head and wonderful horns.

"Some people believe that Bighorn leaps from cliffs and alights on those great horns, but this not true. Whenever he leaps he alights on those sure feet of his, not on his head.

"Way up in the extreme northwest corner of this country, in a place called Alaska, is a close cousin whose coat is all white and whose horns are yellow and more slender and wider spreading. He called the Dall Mountain Sheep. Farther south, but not as far south as the home of Bighorn, is another cousin whose coat is so dark that he is sometimes called the Black Mountain Sheep. His proper name is Stone's Mountain Sheep. In the mountains between these two is another cousin with a white head and dark body called Fannin's sheep. All these cousins are closely related and in their habits are much alike. Of them all, Bighorn the Rocky Mountain Sheep is the best known."

"I should think," said Peter Rabbit, "that way up there on those high mountains Bighorn would be very lonesome."

Old Mother Nature laughed. "Bighorn doesn't care for neighbors as you do, Peter," said she. "But even up in those high rocky retreats among the clouds he has a neighbor as sure-footed as himself, one who stays winter as well as summer on the mountain tops. It is Billy the Rocky Mountain Goat.

"Billy is as awkward-looking as he moves about as Bighorn is graceful, but he will go where even Bighorn will hesitate to follow. His hoofs are small and especially planned for walking in safety on smooth rock and ice-covered ledges. In weight he is about equal to Lightfoot the Deer, but he doesn't look in the least like him.

"In the first place he has a hump on his shoulders much like the humps of Thunderfoot the Bison and Longcoat the Musk Ox. Of course this means that he carries his head low. His face is very long and from beneath his chin hangs a white beard. From his forehead two rather short, slim, black horns stand up with a little curve backward. His coat is white and the hair is long and straight. Under this long white coat he wears a thick coat of short, woolly, yellowish-white fur which keeps him warm in the coldest weather. He seldom leaves his beloved mountain-tops, even in the worst weather of winter, as Bighorn sometimes does, but finds shelter among the rocks. The result is that he has practically no enemies save man to fear.

"Often he spends the summer where the snow remains all the year through and his white coat is a protection from the keenest eyes. You see, when not moving, he looks in the distance for all the world like a patch of snow on the rocks.

"Not having a handsome head or wonderful horns he

has not been hunted by man quite so much as has Bighorn, and therefore is not so alert and wary. Both he and Bighorn are more easily approached from above than from below, because they do not expect danger from above and so do not keep so sharp a watch in that direction. The young are sometimes taken by King Eagle, but otherwise Billy Goat's family has little to fear from enemies, always excepting the hunter with his terrible gun.

"I have now told you of the members of the cattle and Sheep family, what they look like and where they live and how. There is still one more member of the order Ungulata and this one is in a way related to another member of Farmer Brown's barnyard. I will leave you to guess which one. What is it, Peter?"

"If you please, in just what part of the Far West are the mountains where Billy Goat lives?" replied Peter.

"Chiefly in the northern part," replied Old Mother Nature. "In the Northwest these mountains are very close to the ocean and Billy does not appear to mind in the least the fogs that roll in, and seems to enjoy the salt air. Sometimes there he comes down almost to the shore. Are there any more questions?"

There were none, so school was dismissed for the day. Peter didn't go straight home. Instead he went up to the Old Pasture for another look at the old ram there and tried to picture to himself just what Bighorn must look like. Especially he looked at the hoofs of the old ram.

"It is queer," muttered Peter, "how feet like those can be so safe up on those slippery rocks Old Mother Nature told us about. Anyway, it seems queer to me. But it must be so if she says it is. My, my, my, what a lot of strange people there are in this world! And what a lot there is to learn!"

CHAPTER XXXIX
Piggy and Hardshell

All the way to school the next morning Peter Rabbit did his best to guess who it might be that they were to learn about that day. "Old Mother Nature said that he is related to some one who lives in Farmer Brown's barnyard," said Peter to himself. "Now who can it be?" But try as he would, Peter couldn't think of any one. He asked Jumper the Hare if he had guessed who it could be. Jumper shook his head.

"I haven't the least idea," said he. "You know I seldom leave the Green Forest and I never have been over to that barnyard in my life, so of course I don't know who lives there."

Danny Meadow Mouse and Whitefoot the Wood Mouse were no wiser, nor was Johnny Chuck. But Chatterer the Red Squirrel, it was plain to see, was quite sure he knew who it was. Chatterer had been over to Farmer Brown's so often to steal corn from the corn crib that he knew all about that barnyard and who lived there. But though Peter and the others teased him to tell them he wouldn't.

So when Old Mother Nature asked who had guessed to whom she had referred Chatterer was the only one to reply. "I think you must have meant the Pig who is always rooting about and grunting in that barnyard," said he.

"Your guess is right, Chatterer," she replied, smiling at the little red-coated rascal, "and this morning I will tell you a little about a relative of his who doesn't live in a barnyard, but lives in the forest, as free and independent as you are. It is Piggy the Peccary, known as the Collared Peccary, also called Wild Pig, Muskhog, Texas Peccary and Javelina.

"He is a true Pig and in shape resembles that lazy, fat fellow in Farmer Brown's barnyard when he was little. You would know him for a Pig right away if you should see him. But in every other way excepting his habit of rooting up the ground with his nose, he is a wholly different fellow. For

PIGGY THE COLLARED PECCARY. He is called Wild Pig an Muskhog.

one thing his legs, though short, are more slender and he is a fast runner. There isn't a lazy bone in him, and he is too active to grow fat.

"His head is large and his nose long, and his tail is almost no tail at all; it is just a little rounded knob, as if he had at one time had a tail and it had been cut off. His hair is coarse and stiff, the kind of hair called bristles. From the back of his head along his back the bristles are long and stout. They are black at the tips so that he appears to have a black back. When Piggy is angry he raises these long bristles so that they stand straight up and this gives him a very fierce appearance.

"His color is so dark a gray that at a distance he appears black. Indeed he is black on many parts of him. Just back of the neck a whitish band crosses the shoulders, and this is why he is called the Collared Peccary. You see he seems to be wearing a collar. On each jaw are two great pointed teeth called tusks, the two upper ones so long that they project beyond the lips. These tusks are Piggy's weapons, and very good ones they are.

"The home of Piggy the Peccary is in the hot southwestern part of this country, where live Jaguar and Ocelot, the beautiful spotted members of the Cat family. They are two of his enemies. He never likes to be alone, but lives with a band of his friends and they roam about together. He is found on the plains and among low hills, in swamps and dense forests, and among the thickets of cactus and other thorny plants that grow in dry regions. Plenty of food and shelter from the hot sun seem to be the main things with Piggy."

"What does he eat?" asked Peter Rabbit.

Old Mother Nature laughed. "It would be easier, Peter, to tell you what he doesn't eat," said she. "He eats everything eatable, nuts, fruits, seeds, roots and plants of various kinds, insects, Frogs, Lizards, Snakes and any small animals he can catch. Sometimes he does great damage to gardens and crops planted by man. He delights to root in the earth with his nose and often turns over much ground in this way, searching for roots good to eat.

"On the lower part of his back he carries a little bag of musky scent, and from this he gets the name of Muskhog. While as a rule he wisely runs from danger, he is no coward, and will fight fiercely when cornered. His friends at once rush to help him and surround the enemy, who is usually glad to climb a tree to escape their gnashing tusks. However, he is not the fierce animal he has been reported to be, ready to attack unprovoked. He will run away if he can. Mr. and Mrs. Peccary have two babies at a time.

"This is the last of the hoofed animals and the last but one of the land animals of this great country, so you see we are almost to the end of school. This last one is perhaps the queerest of all. It is Hardshell the Armadillo, and belongs to the order of Edentata, which means toothless."

"Do you mean to say that there are animals with no teeth at all?" asked Happy Jack Squirrel, looking as if he couldn't believe such a thing.

Old Mother Nature nodded. "That is just what I mean," said she. "There are animals without any teeth, though not in this country, and others with so few teeth that they have been put in the same order with the wholly toothless ones. Hardshell the Armadillo is one of these. He has no teeth at all in the front of his mouth and such teeth as he has got do not amount to much."

"But why do you call him Hardshell?" asked Peter impatiently.

"Because instead of a coat of fur he wears a coat of shell," replied Old Mother Nature, and then laughed right out at the funny expressions on the faces before her. It was quite clear that Peter and his friends were having hard work to believe she was in earnest. They suspected her of joking.

"Do—do you mean that he lives in a sort of house that he carries with him like Spotty the Turtle?" ventured Peter.

"It is a shell, but not like that of Spotty," explained Old Mother Nature. "Spotty's shell is all one piece, but the Armadillo's shell is jointed, so that he can roll up like a ball.

HARDSHELL THE ARMADILLO. This is the nine-banded Armadillo of the southwest.

Spotty isn't a mammal, as are all of you and all those we have been learning about, but is a reptile. Hardshell the Armadillo, on the other hand, is a true mammal."

"Well, all I can say is that he must be a mighty queer looking fellow," declared Peter.

"He is," replied Old Mother Nature. "He is about the size of Unc' Billy Possum, and if you can imagine a pig of about that size with very short legs, a long tapering tail, feet with toes and long claws and a shell covering his whole body, the front of his face and even his tail, you will have something of an idea what he looks like.

"He lives down in the hot Southwest where Piggy the Peccary lives. His coat of shell is yellowish in color and is divided in the middle of his body into nine narrow bands or joints. Because of this he is called the Nine-banded Armadillo. In the countries to the south of this he has a cousin with three bands and another with six.

"Hardshell's head is very long and he carries it pointed straight down. His small eyes are set far back, and at the top of his head are rather large upright ears. The shell of his tail is divided into many jointed rings so that he can move it at will.

"His tongue is long and sticky. This is so that he can run it out for some distance and sweep up the Ants and insects on which he largely lives. His eyesight and hearing are not very good, and having such a heavy, stiff coat he is a poor runner. But he is a good digger. This means, of course, that he makes his home in a hole in the ground. When frightened he makes for this, but if overtaken by an enemy he rolls up into a ball and is safe from all save those with big and strong enough teeth to break through the joints of his shell. He eats some vegetable matter and is accused of eating the eggs of ground-nesting birds, and of dead decayed flesh he may find. However, his food consists chiefly of Ants, insects of various kinds, and worms. He is a harmless little fellow and interesting because he is so queer. He is sometimes killed and eaten by man and his flesh is considered very good. He has from four to eight babies in the early spring. The baby Armadillo has a soft, tough skin instead of a shell, and as it grows it hardens until by the time it is fully grown it has become a shell.

"Now this finishes the lessons about the land animals or mammals. There are other mammals who live in the ocean, which is the salt water which surrounds the land, and which, I guess, none of you have ever seen. Some of these come on shore and some never do. To-morrow I will tell you just a little about them, so that you will know something about all the animals of this great country which is called North America. That is, I will if you want me to."

"We do! Of course we do!" cried Peter Rabbit, and it is plain that he spoke for all.

CHAPTER XL
THE MAMMALS OF THE SEA

It was the last day of Old Mother Nature's school in the Green Forest, and when jolly, round, bright Mr. Sun had climbed high enough in the blue, blue sky to peep down through the trees, he found not one missing of the little people who had been learning so much about themselves, their relatives, neighbors and all the other animals in every part of this great country. You see, not for anything in the world would one of them willingly have missed that last lesson.

"I told you yesterday," began Old Mother Nature, "that the land is surrounded by water, salt water, sometimes called the ocean and sometimes the sea. In this live the largest animals in all the Great World and many others, some of which sometimes come on land, and others which never do.

"One of those which come on land is first cousin to Little Joe Otter and is named the Sea Otter.

"He lives in the cold waters of the western ocean of the Far North. He much resembles Little Joe Otter, whom you all know, but has finer, handsomer fur. In fact, so handsome is his fur that he has been hunted for it until now. He is among the shyest and rarest of all animals, and has taken to living in the water practically all the time, rarely visiting land. He lies on his back in the water and gets his food from the bottom of the sea. It is chiefly clams and other shellfish. He rests on floating masses of sea plants. He is very playful and delights to toss pieces of seaweed from paw to paw as he lies floating on his back. Of course he is a wonderful swimmer and diver. Otherwise he couldn't live in the sea.

"Another who comes on land, but only for a very short distance from the water, is called the Walrus. He belongs to an order called Finnipedia, which means fin-footed. Instead of having legs and feet for walking, members of this order have limbs designed for swimming; these are more like fins or paddles than anything else and are called flippers. The Walrus is so big that I can give you no idea how big he is, excepting to say that he will weigh two thousand pounds. He is simply a great mass of living flesh covered with a rough, very thick skin without hair. From his upper jaw two immense ivory tusks hang straight down, and with these he digs up shellfish at the bottom of the sea. It is a terrible effort for him to move on shore, and so he is content to stay within a few feet of the water. He also lives in the cold waters of the Far North amidst floating ice. On this he often climbs out to lie for hours. His voice is a deep grunt or bellowing roar. The young are born on land close to the water.

"The Sea Lions belong to this same fin-footed order. The best known of these are the California Sea Lion and the Fur Seal, which is not a true Seal. The California Sea Lion is also called the Barking Sea Lion because of its habit of barking, and is the best known of the family. It is frequently seen on the rocks along the shore and on the islands off the western coast. These Sea Lions are sleek animals, exceedingly graceful in the water. They have long necks and carry their heads high. They are covered with short coarse hair and have small, sharp-pointed ears. Their front flippers have neither hair nor claws, but their hind flippers have webbed toes. They are able to move about on land surprisingly well for animals lacking regular legs and feet, and can climb on and over rocks rapidly. Naturally they are splendid swimmers.

"The largest member of the family is the Steller Sea Lion, who sometimes grows to be almost as big as a Walrus. He is not sleek and graceful like his smaller cousin, but has an enormously thick neck and heavy shoulders. His voice is a roar rather than a bark. The head of an old Sea Lion is so much like that of a true Lion that the name Sea Lion has been given this family.

"The most valuable member of the family, so far as man

is concerned, is the Fur Seal, also called Sea Bear. It is very nearly the size and form of the California Sea Lion, but under the coarse outer hair, which is gray in color, is a wonderful soft, fine, brown fur and for this the Fur Seal has been hunted so persistently that there was real danger that soon the very last one would be killed. Now wise and needed laws protect the Fur Seals on their breeding grounds, which are certain islands in the Far North. The young of all members of this family are born on shore, but soon take to the water. The Fur Seal migrates just as the birds do, but always returns to the place of its birth. Man and the Polar Bear are its enemies on land and ice, and the Killer Whale in the water. Mr. Fur Seal always has many wives and this is true of the other members of the Sea Lion family and of the Walrus. The males are three or four times the size of the females. Among themselves the males are fierce fighters.

"The true Seals are short-necked, thick-bodied, and have rather round heads with no visible ears. The Walrus and Sea Lions can turn their hind flippers forward to use as feet on land, but this the true Seals cannot do. Therefore they are more clumsy out of water. Their front flippers are covered with hair.

"The one best known is the Harbor or Leopard Seal. It is found along both coasts, often swimming far up big rivers. It is one of the smallest members of the family. Sometimes it is yellowish-gray spotted with black and sometimes dark brown with light spots.

"The Ringed Seal is about the same size or a little smaller than the Harbor Seal and is found as far north as it can find breathing holes in the ice. You know all these animals breathe air just as land animals do. This Seal looks much like the Harbor Seal, but is a little more slender.

"Another member of the family is the Harp, Saddle-back or Greenland Seal. He is larger than the other two and has a black head and gray body with a large black ring on the back. The female is not so handsome, being merely spotted.

"The handsomest Seal is the Ribbon Seal. He is about the size of his cousin the Harbor Seal. He is also called the Harlequin Seal. Sometimes his coat is blackish-brown and sometimes yellowish-gray, but always he has a band of yellowish-white, like a broad ribbon, from his throat around over the top of his head, and another band which starts on his chest and goes over his shoulder, curves down and finally goes around his body not far above the hind flippers. Only the male is so marked. This Seal is rather rare. Like most of the others it lives in the cold waters of the Far North.

"The largest of the Seals is the Elephant Seal, once numerous, but killed by man until now there are few members of this branch of the family. He is a tremendous fellow and has a movable nose which hangs several inches below his mouth.

"The queerest-looking member of the family is the Hooded Seal. Mr. Seal of this branch of the family is rather large, and on top of his nose he carries a large bag of skin which he can fill with air until he looks as if he were wearing a queer hood or bonnet.

"The Seals complete the list of animals which live mostly in the water but come out on land or ice at times. Now I will tell you of a true mammal, warm-blooded, just as you are, and air-breathing, but which never comes on land. This is the Manatee or Sea Cow. It lives in the warm waters of the Sunny South, coming up from the sea in the big rivers. It is a very large animal, sometimes growing as big as a medium-sized Walrus. The head is round, somewhat like that of a Seal. The lips are thick and big, the upper one split in the middle. The eyes are small. It has but two flippers, and these are set in at the shoulders. Instead of hind flippers, such as the Seals and Sea Lions have, the Manatee has a broad, flattened and rounded tail which is used as a propeller, just as fish use their tails. The neck is short and large. In the water the Manatee looks black. The skin is almost hairless.

"This curious animal lives on water plants. Sometimes it

will come close to a river bank and with head and shoulders out of water feed on the grasses which hang down from the bank. The babies are, of course, born in the water, as the Manatee never comes on shore. Now I think this will end to-day's lesson and the school."

Peter Rabbit hopped up excitedly. "You said that the largest animals in the world live in the sea, and you haven't told us what they are," he cried.

"True enough, Peter," replied Old Mother Nature pleasantly. "The largest living animal is a Whale, a true mammal and not a fish at all, as some people appear to think. There are several kinds of Whales, some of them comparatively small and some the largest animals in the world, so large that I cannot give you any idea of how big they are. Beside one of these, the biggest Walrus would look like a baby. But the Whales do not belong just to this country, so I think we will not include them.

"Now we will close school. I hope you have enjoyed learning as much as I have enjoyed teaching, and I hope that what you have learned will be of use to you as long as you live. The more knowledge you possess the better fitted for your part in the work of the Great World you will be. Don't forget that, and never miss a chance to learn."

And so ended Old Mother Nature's school in the Green Forest. One by one her little pupils thanked her for all she had taught them, and then started for home. Peter Rabbit was the last.

"I know ever and ever so much more than I did when I first came to you, but I guess that after all I know very little of all there is to know," said he shyly, which shows that Peter really had learned a great deal. Then he started for the dear Old Briar-patch, lipperty-lipperty-lip.

www.ingramcontent.com/pod-product-compliance
Lightning Source LLC
Chambersburg PA
CBHW031543260326
41914CB00002B/243

* 9 7 8 1 9 2 2 6 3 4 6 7 2 *